MW00415114

the humor habit

Foreword by **Jenn Lim**

Paul Osincup

the humor habit

Rewire Your Brain to Stress Less, Laugh More, and Achieve More'er

WILEY

Published by John Wiley & Sons, Inc., Hoboken, New Jersey.
Published simultaneously in Canada.

For general information on our other products and services or for technical support, please contact our Customer Care Department within the United States at (800) 762-2974, outside the United States at (317) 572-3993 or fax (317) 572-4002.

Wiley also publishes its books in a variety of electronic formats. Some content that appears in print may not be available in electronic formats. For more information about Wiley products, visit our web site at www.wiley.com.

Library of Congress Cataloging-in-Publication Data

Names: Osincup, Paul, author.
Title: The humor habit : rewire your brain to stress less, laugh more, and achieve more'er / Paul Osincup.
Description: Hoboken, New Jersey : Wiley, [2024] | Includes index.
Identifiers: LCCN 2023057839 (print) | LCCN 2023057840 (ebook) | ISBN 9781394234356 (hardback) | ISBN 9781394234370 (adobe pdf) | ISBN 9781394234363 (epub)
Subjects: LCSH: Wit and humor—Psychological aspects. | Positive psychology.
Classification: LCC BF575.L3 O756 2024 (print) | LCC BF575.L3 (ebook) | DDC 152.4/3—dc23/eng/20240126
LC record available at https://lccn.loc.gov/2023057839
LC ebook record available at https://lccn.loc.gov/2023057840

Cover Design: Wiley
Cover Image: Coffee Mug © New Africa / Adobe Stock, Napkin © sebra / Adobe Stock
Author Photo: Courtesy of the Author
SKY10068635_022924

They say behind every good man is a great woman.
For me, it took four.
For my mom, Debby; my sisters, Ali and Laurie;
and for my incredible wife, Kelly.

Contents

Foreword

When Paul first asked me to write the foreword for his book I thought, "Oh, great. Do I have to be funny?" Then I realized that in the world of comedy, a headliner wouldn't want the opener to be funnier than them, so I'm happy to temporarily shelve my inner comedienne—you know, for Paul's sake.

The next thought I had was to what do I owe this honor of writing the foreword to *The Humor Habit*, especially at a time we could all use a bit (if not A LOT) more joy and laughter. Since the world got 2020'd, it's taken some time for us to adapt. And as we've consistently seen in Gallup's reports of burnout and stress in the global workforce, I think it's safe to say that most of us still have yet to fully exhale with relief.

With all this talk of doom and gloom, you might be surprised that I've been in the happiness space for 15 years now. I helped launch a bestselling book titled *Delivering Happiness* and became the CEO of the culture consulting company of the same name. We've worked with hundreds of organizations around the world—from Fortune 500s and hospitals, to startups and the government of Dubai—to instill sustainable happiness in its processes and employees. Years later, I launched another bestseller, *Beyond Happiness*, a book and company that's prioritizing how we can all be more human at work (and therefore, life).

I share all of this in the context of how *The Humor Habit* couldn't be timelier and more relevant to our 2024 A.C. (After Covid) world. In my work with individuals and organizations over the past several years, I've observed that people might not want to be happy all the time (and let's be real, it's impossible to be), but no one denies wanting to be true to their *authentic* selves and having a desire to *grow*.

To me, *The Humor Habit* hits both those notes in a way that captures what Paul's purpose is—in this book, in his keynotes and comedy, in his every interaction with people he touches—to positively impact others with practical tools, knowledge, and inspiration. But the best part about his approach is that he does it with his superpower of sprinkling just the right amount of humor in any given situation, with tact and integrity. And it helps that he's damn funny too.

I first met Paul in 2019 at a retreat to become a *Delivering Happiness* certified coach. It was a stellar, experienced group of coaches joining the team, and it made an impression that Paul was selected by the group as the "Culture Champion" who best exemplified the team and organizational values.

Over the years, I've been impressed and entertained working with Paul and seeing him in action. Doing anything with him, whether it was in a meeting or podcast, was always a little more fun. Being known as the company's "funny guy" might seem to be a tall order to live up to, but Paul never disappointed.

Yet, something struck me most when the world got 2020'd with the pandemic, social unrest, climate change, and the umpteen other things that turned our lives inside out. Even when times were rough, when humor might be the last thing on people's minds, there was one thing that stood out in how he navigated it . . . with *discernment*.

During COVID, Paul reminded our team of coach|sultants™ about the value of levity and humor, not just for lightening the mood, but for human connection, well-being, and feeling both a sense of progress and control when VUCA (Volatility Uncertainty Complexity Ambiguity) was relentlessly breathing down our necks. His empathy and sympathy showed in how seriously he took humor as a tool to keep things intentional, fresh, and playful for the greatest impact with our clients.

What also differentiates Paul is that he's not just an academic, but a practitioner too. You'd be shocked to know how many academics in the happiness space are simply *not happy*. I love how Paul keeps walking his talk as a humor expert by making me, the team, and clients laugh and learn at the same time—which is why you're going to love this book. I respect how he weaves his passions of improv and stand-up comedy into his content and delivery, making it obvious he is showing up as his true, authentic self.

It's been a few years since the pandemic, but with the constant drumroll of another news headline that makes us think WHAT THE WHAT?! the world is still a super heavy place. And by reframing the role of humor in our everyday lives, we can learn how to intentionally dial up a more meaningful, enjoyable life as we dial down the noise that just gets in the way.

Being in the science of happiness space for years, we know there are certain habits (like gratitude and optimism) that are tools to make us sustainably happier. I've always considered humor as a byproduct of happiness, but in this book, Paul shows us that it's not a result of happiness, but a means to it—another habit.

These days I'm all about what's *beyond* happiness, and I can't highlight enough what I appreciate most about Paul's approach in this book—it's not about using humor to avoid negative feelings or the shitty parts of life; it's about using it to face them, invite them into your living room, play with them, and learn how humor brings you closer to your authentic self.

I wish everyone could have a miniature-sized Paul they could keep in their back pocket. How cool would it be to have someone who can lighten up the room (even Zoom rooms) and communicate with safety, intention, and impact? While we haven't figured out the tech for cloning or miniaturizing yet, reading this book is the next best thing (and it protects pocket-Paul from being sat on or put through the wash).

So have fun learning, laughing, and developing your own Humor Habit!

Jenn Lim
CEO, Cofounder of Delivering Happiness
Author, CEO, and Founder of Beyond Happiness

Introduction

"I don't want to live my life as an actor in a drama just to reach the end and realize I was the director, and it could have been a comedy."

Do you get stressed out, burned out, or checked out? Do you feel overworked, overcommitted, and overwhelmed by the demands at work and home? If the answer is "no," then thanks for scanning this page, AI bot, and please forward this book on to a human. I wrote this book for anyone who wants to be less stressed and live a little lighter—which really only excludes infants, transcendental philosophers, and Matthew McConaughey.

If you're like me . . . you're 5′4″ and bald. But now that I think of it, that's not really applicable to this book, so let's start over. If you're like me . . . you get stressed out. Sometimes the stress is manageable, maybe even helpful, and other times it's a full-blown freak-out. I speak about humor, happiness, and make people laugh for a living, so I feel like I'm supposed to maintain the image of always being this easy-going, fun, and light-hearted guy. While I do think I am all those things, the truth is, I also have my fair share of freak-outs.

I've screamed into pillows, stomped my feet like a two-year-old, I've even been so stressed I hit myself in the face. I know that sounds weird and it caught me by surprise too (apparently, I've got a jab like Mike Tyson), but at times my stress could get out of control. Even when I wasn't going full toddler Tyson, stress could get the best of me, keeping me up all night worrying about things that were never as big a deal as my brain made them out to be. When I was in graduate school, my doctor told me my stress was so bad, I had developed an arrythmia. I said, "An arrythmia? Oh, don't worry. I've never had rhythm." He was like "No, idiot. Arrythmia is an irregular heartbeat." Man, was I quite the catch—a short, bald, 24-year-old stress case with heart problems . . . and no rhythm.

But I wasn't always such a stress case. In fact, as a kid, humor was a core part of who I was. I loved getting laughs, and even began to see the power of humor at a young age. The first time I remember noticing the influence and effect of humor was in third grade. I was distracting other kids by talking and was promptly yelled at by Mrs. Temple, who glared at me and yelled "Paul, you have diarrhea of the mouth!" Half the class laughed, and the other half went "Ooooohhhh!" because it was a pretty sick burn. Now I was embarrassed, and without thinking, I put my open palm to my bottom lip, looked at Mrs. Temple and said "Aw, sick, it's running down my chin!" That unsophisticated, yet age-appropriate retort earned me a raucous laugh from my classmates . . . and a trip to the principal's office.

The principal asked me what happened, so I told her, "I said something inappropriate in Mrs. Temple's class."

The principal replied, "Tell us what you said."

"Well, she said I had diarrhea of the mouth, so I said, 'Aw, sick, it's running down my chin.'"

The principal and the other staff members in the office laughed. Then they quickly tried to straighten their faces as little smirks were peeking out the corners of their mouths. They couldn't be that mad at me . . . because it was funny! Of course, she collected herself and told me it was inappropriate with a fake stern look on her face, but I knew deep down she was thinking, "Not bad, kid." I knew I had discovered something, and I felt like a Jedi. Not only did the humor soften the blow in the principal's office, but it got me out of the stressful and slightly traumatic situation of being embarrassed by my teacher in front of the whole class.

Fortunately, over time, I learned there are more sophisticated forms of humor than diarrhea jokes. However, what I learned about humor instinctually at a young age, and have now relearned formally as an adult, is that our sense humor is an incredibly powerful feature in the human psyche that can be used intentionally to cope with distress, build relationships, and enhance well-being. It came natural to me as a kid, but somewhere on the road to adulting, I developed a bad case of chronic seriousness that I've been battling ever since. And, after speaking with people all over the world about the benefits of humor and how to use it strategically, I learned that I wasn't alone. Particularly, the past few years have been tough: even as far back as 2015 B.C. (Before Covid), the U.S. surgeon general warned that both stress and isolation were at an all-time high and were two of the most prevalent diseases in America. Now, after navigating a pandemic, we live in a strange new world where we're somehow even more stressed, more isolated, and more likely to clear a room with a cough than a fart. (Okay, perhaps my humor hasn't become fully sophisticated.)

A new reality brings new stressors to add to the pile of original stressors that have been sitting in the corner since 2020 like that old pair of work slacks—the only difference is, the stressors still fit. We need all the coping strategies we can find. For some, traditional mindfulness and stress-reduction strategies like exercise, yoga, or meditation may suffice. But for many, those strategies just aren't enough, aren't the right fit, or require too many essential oils. Here's the good news: In this age of overwhelm, there's an untapped resource we all possess that helps foster connection and boost productivity and enhances our lives—and no, it's not Zoom.

It's our sense of humor.

Don't worry, I'm not just going to review all the research proving that stress is bad and a sense of humor helps. And this book isn't just a bunch of old jokes about the pandemic—because the bad thing about a Covid joke is . . . you don't want people to get it. When we're faced with stress, overwhelm, and trying times, people often say "You just need to have a sense of humor about it" or "Just laugh it off." It's great advice, but the problem is, nobody ever tells us *how* to do that. When am I supposed to laugh things off? When I lock the keys of my rental car in the trunk just before needing to return it to the airport? "Oh, ha, ha, ha, look what I've done! Life is just so silly!" Not realistic. I start to get pissed off, get stressed, and freak out. In this book, I'll provide you with practical strategies for developing your sense of humor into a powerful mindfulness tool. You'll learn specific approaches drawing on cutting-edge positive psychology and neuroscience research combined with timeless techniques from the world of stand-up and improv comedy that will help you freak out less and see the humor in life more.

My stress-induced heart palpitations started to subside toward the end of graduate school right about the time I began performing stand-up comedy, and my life began to change for the better. I met my future wife, lost weight, and got a great new job. Did writing and performing comedy really cure my stress, make me healthier, and make my life better? No. I'm pretty sure I lost weight by simply skipping my midnight "fourth meal" chalupas and there's nothing better for decreasing stress than finishing graduate school. The comedy thing is purely coincidental, although knowing what I know now about the relationship between humor and stress, I'm certain it helped me cope.

My master's degree is in Higher Education Leadership and Policy Studies. (No wonder I was stressed. Policy Studies? Gross.) As my career progressed, my focus narrowed to working with at-risk college students. Specifically, I worked with students who were in trouble with the law. I was a lead member of a multidisciplinary drug and alcohol treatment program for students with substance abuse and co-occurring mental health issues, and I taught graduate courses on communication and conflict resolution. Part of my job included investigating and adjudicating threats to campus including incidents of domestic violence and sexual assault, as well as having difficult conversations with parents, attorneys, and students when a suspension or expulsion was eminent. I worked with college students in some capacity for over 15 years and although it was stressful at times, it was extremely gratifying to watch people turn their lives around in the face of adversity.

I share my prior professional career details so you know that I haven't always just talked humor and comedy for a living, and I have actually had a real job. I understand what it's like to work in a high-stress, high-stakes environment where the decisions you make affect other people's lives.

What became clear to me is that when I became chronically serious, and focused solely on the intensity of the work, my sense of humor began to slowly evaporate. Just like other healthy habits like eating right and exercising can, my humor habit started to crumble under the pressure of stress. I wouldn't watch, write, or perform comedy as much, and before long I noticed my humor muscle begin to atrophy. I couldn't see the humor in life as easily—I was losing my funny focus. During these periods I found myself becoming more negative, always having grievances to bear for the smallest of slights, and becoming fluent in cynicism. I noticed when these changes happened, and although I didn't know how to fix it then, I knew I wanted to because I didn't like that version of me. I remember thinking "I don't want to live my life as an actor in a drama just to reach the end and realize I was the director, and it could have been a comedy."

For years it didn't occur to me that the amount of humor in my life affected my mood, my relationships, and even my work performance. Humor is a mindset—a way of being. As I began dabbling in comedy again, I noticed that the simple act of immersing myself in humor helped me find the necessary perspective to balance the gravity of life with the levity of it.

The more I immersed myself in humor, the more I began to nerd out about it. I started to notice how much I used humor with my staff, colleagues, and students. Sometimes it worked to lighten the mood in the office, or to connect with students and parents. I remember one student who came in with his mom and his attorney to meet with me about an alcohol and vandalism incident. He tried his best to dress up in jeans, a dress shirt that was way too big, and a tie. He was extremely nervous as he drank several cups of water and then anxiously tore the paper cup to tiny little shreds on the table as he was waiting. I always tried to help students chill out a bit by getting to know them. When I asked what his major was he said, "I'm double majoring in Animal Science and Mechanical Engineering."

I said, "Wow, double major, that's impressive! Animal Science and Mechanical Engineering? You could make mechanical bulls!" Okay, it wasn't a great joke, but it was off the cuff, so cut me some slack. The mom snickered, the attorney replied, "That was so bad, it was good," and the student quietly looked up and said, "I think I'm gonna start telling my dad that's why I double majored." The four of us laughed, and I saw the student take a deep breath, sit up in his chair and appear much more at ease.

As my professional career progressed, I became obsessed with learning more about the power of humor and began researching and speaking on the topic. As I learned more about humor, I realized that we can use it intentionally for reasons other than just entertainment. My nerdy humor obsession led to a career merging my inner educator and inner comedian, as I now share laughs and learnings, speaking to professionals all over the world about how to harness the power of humor to enhance their well-being and performance. Everything I've learned from the application of humor as a comedian and from the research as a humor nerd is what led to this book.

We can strategically use humor for communication purposes—to teach, lead, and influence. And we can use humor to enhance overall well-being—increase productivity, elevate performance, boost happiness, foster resilience, and decrease stress. That is what this book is about. I love entertaining people with humor and it's why I still perform comedy, but as I've learned about how essential and beneficial humor is to our well-being, I began to shift my focus from *getting laughs* to *giving laughs*. Speaking on this topic for over a decade, I've accumulated so many tools, tricks, and tips that no matter how long I'm asked to speak or give a workshop, I find I always want to provide the group with more material than will fit into my allotted time. So, I hope I can get all this stuff out of my head and into your hands so you can find ways to leverage levity in your own life.

Now, of course, I chose to be a speaker and not a writer—I LOVE making people laugh and the sound of a room filled with infectious laughter. When I'm in front of an audience I get instant feedback on whether I've done my job. In writing, however, the only sound I hear is my keyboard clacking and my yellow Labrador retriever Bridger snoring under my desk. There may be times when I try to make you laugh and fail, or times when I'm not trying to be funny and you smile or laugh anyway—but I may never know. Have you already laughed? I'm not sure, but I do know it still sounds like someone is under my desk blowing an air hose through a meatloaf. So, there's that.

I'm writing this book, not from a desire to be an author, but because I believe:

1. Humor and laughter are good for our mental and physiological health.
2. Humor can be used intentionally and strategically for desired outcomes.
3. **Humor is not a talent. Humor is a habit.** Yes, there are people with the talent to do impersonations or who may be naturally quick witted, but everyone can develop their sense of humor, learn to use humor more effectively, and see the humor in life more often.

In an age where artificial intelligence bots are being trained with skills to assume the roles of humans, one thing they can't replicate is the human sense of humor.[1] You've been developing your unique sense of humor since you were a kid sharing laughs with your siblings, your best friend, or your invisible friend. Your sense of humor is your personalized brand of funny—your distinctive view of the world, and it can be enhanced and developed as a productivity and leadership tool. If you don't want to be replaced by a robot, then don't act like one. One day it will be your sense of humor that separates you from the machines.

At work or outside of work, we're all struggling with something in our lives that others may know nothing about. And on some days, resilience comes a lot easier than on others. They say "When life gives you lemons, make lemonade," but have you ever tasted lemonade made from just lemons? It's crap. It's sour. It's a glass of citric acid. To make lemonade, you need those crappy lemons life gave you as well as something sweet. Humor is life's sweetener. The great thing is, it's your life so you get to choose when, what kind, and how much sweetener to use at any given moment. This book is here to show you how to create your own endless supply of sweeteners to have at the ready for life's lemons so you can continue to fill your cup, and maybe one day open your own lemonade stand to share with others.

Ultimately, this is about your happiness. We often put too many obstacles into when we can start being happy. "I'll grind through the week, and then this weekend I can have fun and be happy." Or "Once I get a new job or promotion then I'll be successful and that will make me happy." There's no research that tells us this is how happiness works. In fact, there's an array of research tells us it's the other way around. Success does not lead to happiness. Your happiness will lead to your success.[2] Overarching happiness isn't living a life absent of other emotions. Broad-scale happiness is more like the concept of climate versus weather. The climate in Arizona is overall hot and dry, however, the weather on any given day could be cool or rainy. While there will always be sad, frustrated, and angry "weather" moments in our lives, the more happy or joyful "weather" moments we can experience, the more it alters the overall climate of our psyche toward happy. The intentional use of humor is a way to create more joyful "weather" events to impact your climate, and research shows that people who engage in positive humor in their daily lives are happier and more optimistic.[3]

How to Use This Book

This is the part where, if you're standing at the bookstore or previewing the book online wondering if you should buy it, I'm supposed to tell you what it will be like. What's the overall vibe? Is there a roadmap or a blueprint? Honestly, I often skip the introductions of books, so if you've read this far—thank you! That being said, if you know you're going to read this book cover to cover then you can probably skip to Chapter 1 now because I'm just going to let people know what they're in for. If you're still reading, then you're either truly undecided (no pressure, but seriously just read it), or you're a true high achiever "type A" who doesn't want to miss a thing (in which case . . . gold star!)

Combatting Chronic Seriousness (Chapter 1)

We'll take a look at the epidemic of seriousness, the cost of workplace stress, and dip our toes into the fine art of balancing our professional side with our playful side. There's even a fun assessment to take at the end . . . if there's such a thing as a fun assessment.

Let's Geek Out on the Research! (Why Humor Helps) (Chapter 2)

Look, it's up to you. You can just trust me that humor helps you live longer, improves your memory, and makes you fly. Or, you can double-check my research on these things. This is the chapter full of humor facts that will make you sound smart at dinner parties or justify to your boss why watching Tik-Toks before your sales meeting actually optimizes productivity.

Improv(e) Your Mindset (Chapter 3)

This chapter is about getting your mind primed for humor and getting out of the logical, planning, executive functioning part of your brain and into the more creative parts necessary to play with humor. You'll also learn how to turn life's mistakes into gifts and use the principles of improv comedy as a way of life.

Cultivate and Consume (Chapter 4)

This chapter is packed full of strategies for how to stack the deck in your favor to start experiencing humor by choice and not by chance each day. From productivity breaks, to involving friends, and taking control of your social media feeds, you'll get more out of your screen time and literally learn how to laugh more often.

Develop a Funny Focus (Chapter 5)

Have you ever been thinking about getting a new car, and now everywhere you go all you see is that type of car? This chapter is all about how to make that same thing happen, but instead of seeing hatchbacks, you're seeing humor everywhere. Everyone has that one friend who just seems to live a little lighter and always sees the fun and funny side of things. The tools in this chapter are designed to make you that friend.

Bringing Humor to Work with L.A.F.T.E.R.

In these chapters you'll learn specific strategies for the application of humor in a professional environment using the six-step L.A.F.T.E.R. model.

Lead by Example (Chapter 6)

How to incorporate humor in your leadership style and be the spark that ignites the funny flame at work.

Ask for Help (Chapter 7)

If you're not feeling funny or don't have the time, this chapter provides a variety of ways to get help with humor.

Fun over Funny (Chapter 8)

Fun is literally 60% of funny, so it's a great place to start. You'll get real examples of companies using fun at work, the "Fundamentals of Fun" and over 100 ideas for fun you can try.

Tell Your Story (Chapter 9)

How even serious businesses incorporate humor into their marketing, websites, job descriptions, chat bots—and how you can too.

Earn It (Chapter 10)

With great humor, comes great responsibility. We'll cover how to use humor positively, what to do if you have a funny fail, and how to avoid being "that person."

Rituals (Chapter 11)

This chapter highlights the importance of creating consistency in humor and fun for maximum impact on your work culture.

Take Your Pain and Play with It: Using Humor to Boost Resilience (Chapter 12)

This is where we really put humor to the test. You will learn how people have used humor to persevere through the darkest of times, and how to wrap your pain in humor to laugh through adversity. You'll have comedic exercises and formulas to follow as you mine your own pain points for nuggets of humor.

You don't need to be a comedian to benefit from the humor habit; in fact, you don't even need to be funny! All you need to do is strengthen your funny bones by rewiring your brain to see the humor in everyday life. Don't worry; training your brain is easier than training a puppy and shouldn't result in a stained carpet (if it does, you've made yourself laugh too hard). I'm officially passing the mic to you. This is your stage time. Your book. Your humor habit. Your life.

1 Combatting Chronic Seriousness

If you read the book introduction, you already know about my brief trip to the principal's office in elementary school. I swear I wasn't a troublemaker or a bad kid. In fact, I was a good student and an average kid who loved to play outside. Throughout elementary school, I wore one of two shirts every day. My red and white reversible mesh soccer jersey or my No. 81 Steve Watson Denver Broncos jersey. To accompany these fashion choices, I wore gray sweatpants with large holes in both knees surrounded by grass and dirt rings that had set into the fabric from repeated recess soccer and football games. It never occurred to me that I should or would care what other people thought of my appearance. I didn't choose my outfit for any reason other than I knew I'd be playing sports at recess, and this was the gear for an 11-year-old, 4-foot-tall, 50-pound, high-performance athlete like me.

In sixth grade, however, something happened that proved to be the launching point of my professional career . . . I ran for Glennon Heights Elementary Student Council President. To this day, I have no clue where the idea to become a politician came from as I wasn't really seen as that kid. I just don't think I put out very "presidential" vibes. I do recall having fun campaigning and knowing I wouldn't win because I was running against Shanele, the most popular girl in school. With no pressure to win, when it came time to give our speech to the entire school, I decided to perform a rap about why I should be student council president. Man, I wish I remembered or had kept the lyrics to it. Whatever they were, I'm sure it captured all the prepubescent angst and street cred of a Punky Brewster & Ricky Schroder after-school special. (If you were born after 1983, you can google Punky and Ricky—and after-school specials.)

Perhaps it was due to the unsophisticated political acumen of children, or because I was ahead of my time in the rap game, but somehow, I won! So, what is the first thing the Student Council President says when he gets home after being elected (see Figure 1.1)?

Just like that, I had gone from a grass-stained, sports-obsessed rapper to thinking "I'm in a leadership role now and I'm going to have to be taken seriously." What a drama queen. Nobody told me I needed to change my appearance, but for some reason I knew. I knew nobody would take me seriously in my new role if I were dressed like a slob, and I wanted so badly to be respected and to do a good job. That day began a lifelong dilemma that all of us face—how much do I need to be serious, worry about what other people think of me, and how much can I just chill and be myself?

Realistically, to achieve goals like college, graduate school, getting a good job, having a family, and getting promotions, we do need to take things seriously and be taken seriously. But we also all still have our fun, childlike, goofy side that is unique to us, and when accessed, provides healthy perspective and stress relief. Think of it as your CEO versus your inner child. Unfortunately, when we hit age 23, our CEO slaps our inner child's juice box out of their hand, stomps on it, and puts them in "time out" . . . for 50 years. Seriously, a Gallup poll of over 1.4 million people in 166 countries found that our propensity to laugh or smile each day nosedives dramatically around the age of 23, and we don't begin to recover until our mid-seventies. That's 50 years of chronic seriousness![1]

If you have kids—or ever were a kid—it's pretty obvious that they act silly, laugh, and play more than adults do. Kids laugh at the simplest stuff too—it always blows my mind how a three-year-old can

FIGURE 1.1 Photo of me in sixth grade. "Mom, I think I'm gonna need a suit."

laugh for a minute straight at me pretending to hit my head for the eighth time in a row. Even little babies laugh, which is insane. Every time I see a baby laughing I think, "Baby, why are you laughing? You don't even know what funny is yet." They laugh because it's natural and feels good. At least, that's what I tell myself because when a baby looks at my face and just starts laughing I think, "Yeah . . . they must just laugh because it feels good." Either that, or I've met a lot of incredibly rude babies. But from the time we're little laughing rude babies until the time we enter the workforce, we develop a fun, lighthearted, and carefree part of our personality.

Unfortunately, somewhere between college graduation day and our first new employee orientation, we feel the pressure to water down—if not completely mute—that part of who we are. Suddenly, everything we do becomes extremely important as we've gone from playground slides to PowerPoint slides and from soccer practices to best practices. Chronic seriousness begins to creep in as the culture of work demands that we showcase how confident, competent, and capable we are so we can get more leads, get more sales, and get a promotion. Even the way we talk about work has become more intense. We're sucking down quad shot lattes and wheatgrass smoothies and talking to each other like:

> *"I gotta **jump** on a call, then I have a **hard stop**, and gotta **run** to a meeting, so **shoot** me an email, and we'll **tackle** that, **drill down** and **hammer out** the details! We'll deliver the **actionables** and take action on the **deliverables**, have a **tiger team** do a SWOT analysis because there's a lot of **balls in the air** and **irons in the fire**, so we'll **cast a wider net** and **run it up the flagpole**, take a **deep dive**, and see if we can **move the needle**, so keep **grinding**, **hustling**, **crushing**, and **killing it** and we'll all **circle back** while we **Zoom**!"*

It's exhausting, and ultimately, our day-to-day life begins to feel more like a suspenseful drama than a comedy. Every decision feels burdensome, and every adversity catastrophic.

I call it chronic seriousness; you may call it stress. Most of us have a pretty good idea what stress is, and everyone has experienced it—literally from the day we're born. Seriously, that must be one of the most stressful days of our lives. One minute you're cozy and warm, then the next minute everything is cold, bright, and people are up in your grill trying to get a selfie with you.

From delivery-room selfies to boardroom downsizing, we've all encountered plenty of stress in our post-womb experience. Not surprisingly, the workplace seems to be a major culprit. Some industries or companies believe they thrive on the intense, high-pressure, and fast-paced environment. While pressing people to produce better, faster, and longer may heed short-term results, there are hidden costs for those organizations.

Stress: The Hidden Costs to Show Your Boss

- High-pressure companies spend almost 50% more on healthcare costs than other organizations.[2]
- Workplace stress costs the U.S. economy 550 million workdays and more than $500 billion per year.[3]
- 60–80% of workplace accidents are attributed to stress, and it's estimated that more than 80% of doctor visits are due to stress.[4]
- A study of over 3,000 employees showed a significant link between leadership behavior and stress leading to heart disease in employees.[5] (Be careful how you share this one with your boss).

According to research,
your leadership style
is literally killing me.

Leadership behavior can lead to heart disease in employees

- Stress leads to nearly a 50% increase in employee turnover, which is about twice the U.S. national average and the cost to replace those employees is conservatively estimated at one half to two times their annual salary.[6,7]

What's insane is that most of the preceding stressful stats were from before the global Covid-19 pandemic, and unfortunately, it seems to have gotten worse. In North America, workplace stress is a scourge. In Gallup's State of the Global Workplace Report, U.S. and Canadian workers ranked highest for daily stress levels of all groups surveyed. Some 57% of U.S. and Canadian workers reported feeling stress daily, up by 8% from the year prior. Still, 43% of people worldwide are feeling workplace stress and 41% worry daily.[8] The Harris Poll on behalf of the American Psychological Association (APA) found that 3 in 5 (60%) say the number of issues America faces is overwhelming to them.[9] So unless you're still in the womb (in which case—great job learning to read!), you can probably relate to some of this data.

Whether it's a freak-out, stress, compassion fatigue, or burnout, you know the feeling when you have nothing left. My niece had a specific term for her threshold. I was at my sister's house when my niece, who was in high school, got a phone call around 10 p.m. Her friend reminded her of a homework assignment she forgot about that was due the next day. Her face got red, she let out a big sigh and said, "Oh, my god, I can't even . . ." I asked, "What's wrong? Can't even what?" She replied in her best teenage girl stereotype "Ugh, nothing Uncle Paul, I just can't even!" and stomped away. Her mom asked me, "What's wrong with her?" and I said, "I don't know. But whatever it is, it's affected her ability to complete a sentence." Ultimately, the goal is to combat chronic seriousness in order to prevent and manage stress, burnout, compassion fatigue, or the real danger zone where you could be suffering from all three (Figure 1.2).

But seriously, as you make your way through the book learning about how to enhance your sense of humor and use it more intentionally, just remember Figure 1.2, and think about it as a tool to lower your stress load by increasing your capacity to . . . even.

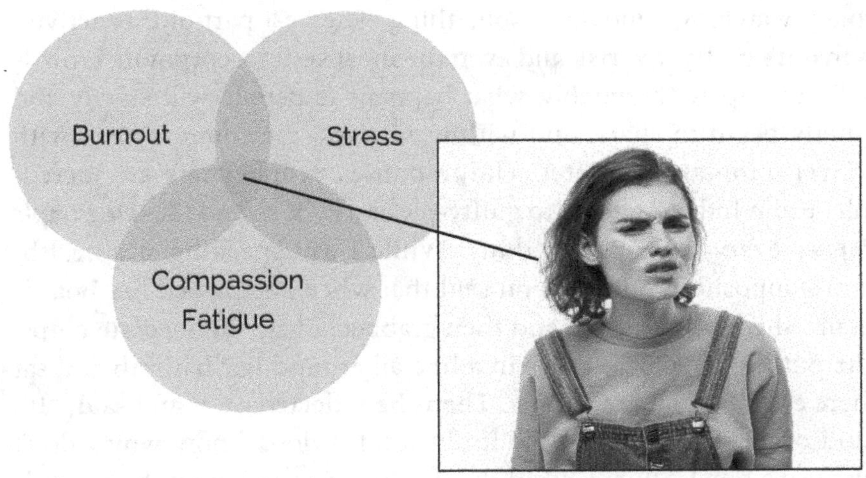

FIGURE 1.2 The stress, burnout, and compassion fatigue danger zone—"Literally Can't Even!"

I'm not going to preach throughout this book that you should just act goofy at work and carry a rubber chicken around or just laugh it off when your kid is misbehaving. We still have to balance being seen as credible versus comical, serious versus silly, professional versus playful, an authority versus . . . an alliteration addict. For real, how many of those did we need there? You get the point. It isn't about just acting like a kid or a clown. It's about the ability to tap into a different mindset more often to break the pattern of overthinking, worry, perfectionism, and planning going on in the prefrontal cortex of your brain.

One brief exercise I do with clients to get them into a less serious mindset during workshops and presentations is something I call "Guilty Pleasure." I simply ask participants to share "a guilty pleasure you have that you don't tell many others about, something weird about you that you love, or something weird that makes you happy." For example, something weird that makes me happy is that I love the smell of my dogs' feet. I know, it's gross and weird—but they smell like Fritos corn chips, I swear! Plus, that smell reminds me of comfort. If I'm smelling that, it probably means I'm cozy on the couch watching a movie or something. The best part of this activity is that it's pretty low risk and even the most serious corporate crowds will participate. Inevitably, what happens is people will slowly and quietly begin to share, and within minutes, the room is alive with conversation and laughter. The responses people share are incredible. From hidden talents to guilty-pleasure TV shows like *Dr. Pimple Popper,* everyone has their thing. While I was speaking at a healthcare symposium, one surgeon said that when she passed her Boards exam, she poured a bath and then grabbed a bag of chocolate chips. She put the chocolate chips in a line all around her bathtub and sat there eating them one by one. Then she reflected on it and said, "It's kind of gross now that I say it out loud. I don't know why I don't just use a bowl." But she said that to this day that's how she rewards herself. Her fellow healthcare colleagues found it hilarious.

An activity like this isn't just to break the ice or to take up time in a long workshop. In fact, a study shared from *Harvard Business Review* highlights how an activity like this can actually boost productivity and performance. The study randomly assigned 93 managers from a variety of industries to teams and asked them to produce creative solutions to a problem. Half the teams were given a warm-up exercise prompt to share about a time they felt pride, while the other half's warm-up exercise was to share embarrassing stories. The "embarrassing story" teams generated 26% more ideas spanning 15% more use categories than their counterparts.[10] There's something magical that happens when we can get into a different mindset, breaking the serious professional barrier just a little, showing more of our true selves. Chances are I'm not going to be as shy about sharing my "outside the box" creative solution with the team after I've just shared that I smell my dogs' feet or eat chocolate chips off the side of my bathtub.

The good news about combatting chronic seriousness is: you're already doing it. Right now you could be planning the weekly grocery list, preparing that work presentation for next week, or reading a more "serious" book. Simply by choosing to read this book as opposed to many other important things you could be doing, you've chosen a less serious and (hopefully) more fun alternative. Think of this book as something fun you're doing for yourself. You know, the whole "putting on your own oxygen mask first before you can be of help to others" metaphor. It's an overused but easily forgotten concept that actually becomes clearer through a kid's mind. I was on a flight to Baltimore sitting next to a little girl and her mom when the captain made the announcement, "If we lose cabin pressure, place the oxygen mask on yourself first before assisting small children." The little girl asked her mom, "Why do they say to put your mask on first?" The patient mom responded, "Why do you think?" The little girl pauses and then just matter-of-factly looks at her mom and says "Cuz you can't help me if you're dead!" The mom and I both chuckled, but this little girl got the concept that we so often forget! I was on a Southwest flight once and the captain said "If you're traveling with a small child, secure your mask first. If you're traveling with more than one child, decide which kid you love most and assist that one first." I'm glad I wasn't sitting next to that family.

To be honest, I don't even believe 100% in this mask metaphor. You don't need to set the bar that high. I don't think it's realistic to always take care of yourself first. There are times when friends, colleagues, pressing work projects, or even the kid we love second most, needs to come first. The problem is that many of us forget to put our mask on at all. The most important thing is to remember to put your own mask on at some point.

Finding ways to combat the chronic seriousness we get so caught up in is crucial to our overall well-being and happiness, but don't just take my word for it. Let's hear from the experts . . . old people. In her book *The Top Five Regrets of the Dying*, palliative care nurse Bronnie Ware interviewed people in hospice within the final three months of their lives. After compiling all the interviews, she found these five common themes emerged as the top five regrets of the dying:[11]

I wish I'd had the courage to live a life true to myself, not the life others expected of me.

I wish I hadn't worked so hard.

I wish I had the courage to express my feelings.

I wish I had stayed in touch with my friends.

I wish that I had let myself be happier.

Which of these hits closest to home for you? "I wish I'd let myself be happier," sticks out for me. I don't want to get to the end and find out that most of my happiness had been a choice and I simply chose to be stuck in old patterns. Ware said that this was surprisingly common and that "Fear of change had them pretending to others, and to their selves, that they were content, when deep within, they longed to laugh properly and have silliness in their life again."[12] We pay a lot of attention to and attempt to develop parts of our personalities like our intellect, drive, ambition, productivity, confidence, empathy, and independence. It's crucial not to take the goofy, funny, silly, childlike part of us—our sense of humor—for granted.

So, about the "Humor Homework"

At the end of most chapters in the book, you'll have homework/activities/exercises/prompts/tasks/projects/whatever name you want to give them that will make you feel accomplished. The book and the Humor Homework are designed to go in a general order:

1. Get yourself into a less serious mindset.
2. Immerse yourself in humor.
3. Train your brain to have a "funny focus" and see humor more often.
4. Use humor at work or in leadership.
5. Use humor to build resilience and cope with adversity.

If you're a high achiever and/or a rule follower, you may feel compelled to complete each activity prior to moving on to the next chapter. That works great. It also works to complete one or two, move on to the next chapter, and come back later to work on other prompts.

This is your book now. No rules. You're an adult and you can do whatever you want. Seriously, you can put whip cream on your coffee this morning—no one is checking.

Humor Homework

Combatting Chronic Seriousness

Your first opportunity to combat chronic seriousness is to take a completely made-up assessment where the answers and scores mean nothing and don't affect your grade or performance review.

How Much Can You "Even"?

Circle the answer that best describes you. Go with your gut and don't overthink it—that's something someone who couldn't "even" would do.

At bedtime I:

A. Sleep like a baby
B. Sleep like a baby spider monkey
C. Lie there analyzing the two-minute conversation I had with the barista this morning and wondering if they thought I was awkward. Then overanalyze the rest of my day.
D. Bedtime? Your privilege is showing.

I would rate my level of focus as:

A. A bald eagle eyeing a trout
B. A bald senior searching for their hat
C. A field mouse on Sudafed
D. When do we get to the humor chapters?

I would say I feel overwhelmed . . .

A. Rarely.
B. A couple of times a month
C. Just on the days that end in *y*
D. Dude, how long is this quiz? I've got crap to do!

How often do you turn to unhealthy food indulgences or drinking excessively when you're overwhelmed?

A. I'll admit, I sneak an occasional cookie
B. Seriously, who brought this person?
C. I already told you . . . the days that end in *y*
D. I'm drunk right now

Do you feel like withdrawing from family and friends, and isolating?

A. I need some occasional alone time
B. Have you met my family?
C. It's hard to read this under my blanket in the closet.
D. You think I'm going to answer that and let you get to know me?

Do you feel irritable, angry, or annoyed over trivial issues?

A. I rarely get angry
B. Again, have you met my family?
C. It's ridiculous that some of these quiz answers have punctuation and others don't. Seriously, get it together.
D. What the hell type of question is that? COME AT ME, BRO!

How Much Can You "Even"?

Self-Score Sheet

When you've finished the assessment, simply add up your answers using the following scoring:

For all *A* answers: 1 point

For all *B* answers: 2 points

For all C answers: 3 points

For all *D* answers: 4 points

If you scored

6–9

Either you're not being honest with yourself, you're being held captive and need to appear fine (blink twice if that's correct), or . . . Congratulations, you can actually "even"!

10–14

You're white knuckling it at times, but surviving. You can "even" on even days, but you can't "even" on odd days. Some activities in this book should help you even the odds.

15–18

Oh. My. Gawd . . . You. Literally. Can't. Even.

19–24

You're odd.

Thanks for having a little fun and taking the **"How Much Can You 'Even'" Assessment**. If you scored as *"Literally Can't 'Even'"* or *"Odd,"* then you'll have plenty of material to draw from in future chapters of this book as we talk about finding humor in the difficult parts of life.

If you thought, *"This is a waste of time"* and skipped the assessment, I get it. Why waste your time with ridiculous nonsense when you can get straight to the substance like tips and strategies? My brain does that to me too. When I take a yoga class, at the end when we're in *savasana* (rest pose) and supposed to let ourselves relax for a few minutes, all I can think is, *"If I get up now, I can get a head start out of here and get a few things done before work."* My yoga instructor told me *"If you don't have time to simply relax for two minutes, then you should make it four."* I don't have another ridiculous assessment for you, but you can always complete this one twice.

2 Let's Geek Out on the Research! (Why Humor Helps)

Whoever said "Laughter is the best medicine" clearly never had diarrhea. Or urinary incontinence. Or cracked ribs. Or severe hemorrhoids. Or the need for . . . actual medicine. For example, when comedian Jim Gaffigan's wife Jeannie was diagnosed with a brain tumor they mentioned how much humor helped her and the family cope with her serious condition.[1] However, they didn't decide to ignore it and have Jim just start telling her jokes every morning. They took it seriously and she spent several weeks in the hospital getting it successfully treated and removed. If laughter really was the best medicine, then how could a comedy writer and wife of a comedian even develop a brain tumor? Also, we know laughter isn't the best medicine because it's still free. My logic is clearly flawless on this topic—no further questions, your honor.

I'm not going to insult you with outrageous claims of humor curing cancer or resolving clinical depression. We'll continue to let 9 out of 10 doctors agree on whatever truly is the best medicine. Humor and laughter, however, are incredible complements to medicine and wellness practices because of the variety of health benefits they produce.

Norman Cousins, a political journalist who won the United Nations Peace Medal in 1971, was one of the first to study the effects of humor on the quality of life. He was diagnosed with ankylosing spondylitis (which I figured from the name caused one to lose their ankles, but it turns out it's a painful degenerative disease in the spine . . . and I shouldn't become a doctor). Cousins became concerned about the amount of pain killers and anti-inflammatories he was ingesting. He understood that negative emotions can adversely affect a patient's health and recovery, but began to wonder if the inverse may be true. Could positive emotions aid in his recovery? With a doctor on board, he developed his own treatment program that included large doses of humor—specifically watching comedy movies in his hospital bed and laughing out loud at them. They discovered decreases in his sedimentation rate (and likely increases in jealous neighboring patients), which meant his inflammation was subsiding.[2] Cousins went on to chronicle his findings in the book *Anatomy of an Illness* and established a Humor Research Task Force to pursue clinical research on humor at UCLA Medical School.

Since Cousins's initial discoveries, researchers have continued to investigate the effects of humor on health and well-being. In fact, that whole "laughing decreasing his inflammation" claim? Yep, we have confirmed studies since then—that's a thing.[3] So next time you've got a swollen knee perhaps instead of *Aleve,* have . . . *a laugh.* (Nothing against Aleve as a brand, it was just the best anti-inflammatory drug to go with the witty alliteration.) Other options for the joke:

- Bufferin—Laugherin
- Ibuprofin—I be laughin'
- Naprosin—Ha-prosin
- Motrin—JokeTrin

See what I mean? These are horrible. "*A laugh* instead of *Aleve*" was the only choice.

There are a multitude of ways that humor helps the mind and body; however, before you completely geek out on the data, it's also important to delineate the difference between humor and laughter.

Humor is "that quality which appeals to a sense of the ludicrous or absurdly incongruous: a funny or amusing quality." Or "a characteristic or habitual disposition or bent: temperament (being in good humor)."[4]

Laughter is: "to show emotion (such as mirth, joy, or scorn) with a chuckle or explosive vocal sound."[5]

Essentially, humor is finding something funny or amusing, and laughter is the physical manifestation of humor in the body. We can, however, make ourselves laugh without finding something funny. While self-induced laughter may not be a result of finding something funny, I believe that doing so still appeals to our sense of the ludicrous, is absurdly incongruous, and is done in good humor.

This is my long-winded way of saying that *while all humor may not evoke laughter, most laughter is sparked by humor*. I say *most* so we exclude nervous laughter, drug-induced laughter, and evil movie villain laughter.

Some Benefits of Humor

When we find something funny or when we laugh, our brains are flooded with a dose of feel-good chemicals.[6,7] By *dose*, I literally mean D.O.S.E.

Dopamine—helps us feel pleasure, rewarded, and motivated.

Oxytocin—helps us connect, feel empathy, and trust.

Serotonin—helps regulate anxiety, happiness, and well-being.

Endorphins—helps reduce pain and stress, boost mood and self-esteem.

So why not use that dose of good stuff to deal with all the doses of bad stuff that happen in our lives? Researchers compared the behaviors of people who use humor to deal with stress (i.e., a humor habit) to those who don't.[8] Here's what their study revealed about *people who cope with stress using humor*.

Humor Makes You More Optimistic

Those with a humor habit were . . .

. . . which short
guys like me are
grateful for

- Twice as likely to find a silver lining in negative situations and appreciate the little things in life.
- More than three times as likely to find beauty all around them.
- 44% less likely to get upset over minor issues.
- Complain 50% less than nonhumor users.
- 71% are mostly or very satisfied with their jobs (vs. 52% of nonhumor users).

Humor Boosts Resilience

Those with a humor habit were . . .

- Twice as likely to see obstacles as temporary and that their problems can be resolved.
- 61% believe it's possible to completely overcome the negative impact of a traumatic experience (vs. 43% of nonhumor users).
- 81% view hardship as an opportunity to learn, grow, and become stronger and wiser (vs. 46% of nonhumor users).
- Twice as likely to push themselves to overcome their fears.
- Take half as many sick days as nonhumor users.

Based on this data, even if you struggle applying the humor habits in this book at first, you'll still be optimistic that you'll persevere! Here are some more funny facts about humor:

Humor Provides a Brain Boost

Researchers at Loma Linda University found that older adults who watched funny videos enjoyed a 23% increase in memory recall.[9]

Various studies have shown that consuming humor as well as having a well-developed *sense of humor enhances one's ability to solve problems and find creative solutions.*[10,11]

That's it. I'm introducing a new bill to start every session of congress with stand-up comedy.

People who watched funny videos boosted their memory recall by 23%.

Wait, did I already say that one? I forgot. I need to go watch some funny TikToks.

Humor Reduces Stress

Even when people experience a similar amount of everyday problems, *those with a well-developed sense of humor will experience less stress* and will be more likely to use positive reappraisal and problem-solving strategies.[12]

In one study, women were given math tests with one group having the added stress of being stereotyped that they were not intelligent enough to perform well. *Women with a higher coping sense of humor responded with less stress and anxiety and performed better overall.*[13]

Wow, humor could be the best weapon against man-splaining! (I think I just man-splained this).

A humor training program studied at two Austrian universities proved effective in *decreasing perceived stress, depressiveness, and anxiety whilst increasing coping humor, cheerfulness, and well-being.*[14]

Humor Improves Immunity

When we laugh, our muscles tighten, causing the body to start producing disease-fighting cells called T cells. Numerous studies have found that laughter and/or watching funny videos *increases T cell production.*[15,16,17]

It works so well, they've renamed them T-hee-hee-hee cells.

Humor Helps Us Live Longer

People who watched one hour of funny material every day after having a heart attack reduced their risk of recurrence, and risk of death by any cause was significantly higher in subjects who laughed less than once a week than in people who laughed more than once per week.[18,19]

You're literally risking your life by not laughing weekly.

Researchers asked healthy adults to watch a humorous 30-minute video or a documentary. The humor video group had significant improvement in their artery function and flexibility that lasted almost 24 hours after watching the video.[20]

Either humor really helps the heart or that documentary was terrible.

Humor Decreases Pain

After completing a humor therapy program, nursing home residents reported *significant decreases in pain* and perception of loneliness, and significant increases in happiness and life satisfaction.[21]

Numerous studies of humor interventions in clinical settings like dialysis and chemotherapy are shown to *increase pain tolerance.*[22,23]

A University of Zurich study testing the *effects of humor on pain thresholds* had participants hold their hands in buckets of ice water and found that humor helped.[24]

My friends conducted a similar study on me at summer camp. In that study the subject peed his pants.

Humor Decreases Burnout and Increases Work Engagement

In a meta-analysis of humor research, the overall trends show that employee humor leads to "enhanced work performance, satisfaction, group cohesion, and coping effectiveness, as well as decreased burnout, stress and work withdrawal." When the boss uses humor, it's "associated with increases in employee work performance, satisfaction, perception of the supervisor's performance, satisfaction with the supervisor, and group cohesion as well as reduced work withdrawal."[25]

. . . which in the meta-verse will just be called . . . an analysis.

Humor Increases Social Connection

Researchers had people watch film clips while connected via video chat with strangers. Even without talking, *those who laughed with the stranger reported far higher levels of liking that person and wanting to get to know them.*[26]

Although I still don't recommend just laughing into the screen on your first video chat with your Tinder match.

In Finland, scientists used PET scans to monitor participants' brain activity during social laughter and found it to be *critical to reinforcing and maintaining social bonds between people.*[27]

On a related note, wild animals can't monitor human brain activity, but PET scan.

While we're at it . . . dogs can't see inside your body, but CAT scan.

Okay, I'll stop.

Humor interventions seem to complement traditional treatment and well-being strategies so well, you'd think doctors would begin prescribing it.

While it's not exactly dosed out like that, believe it or not, there's beginning to be a movement toward humor prescriptions.

R_xs for LOLs

How cool would it be to have humor as part of your recommended treatment plan? Instead of physical therapy, it would be physical comedy therapy—just watching a bunch of Jim Carrey or Melissa McCarthy movies and episodes of *The Three Stooges*. Aside from a prescription for a massage, that's about as good as it gets!

Dosing out dopamine.

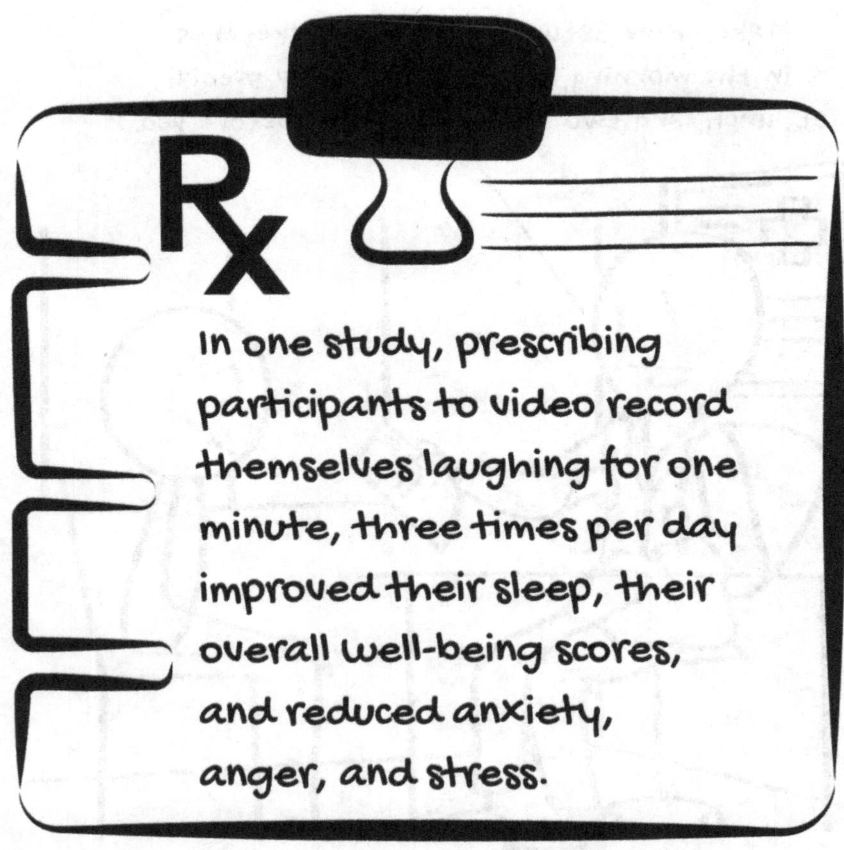

FIGURE 2.1 R_x for a "Laughie." (Adapted from [28])

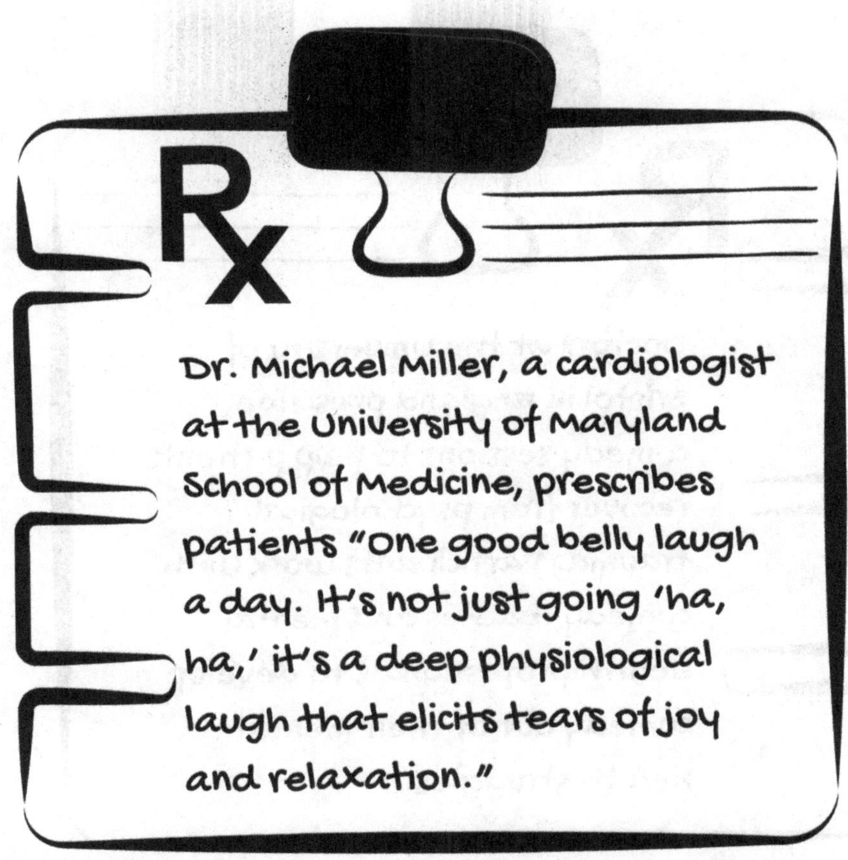

FIGURE 2.2 R_x for a deep belly laugh. (Adapted from[29])

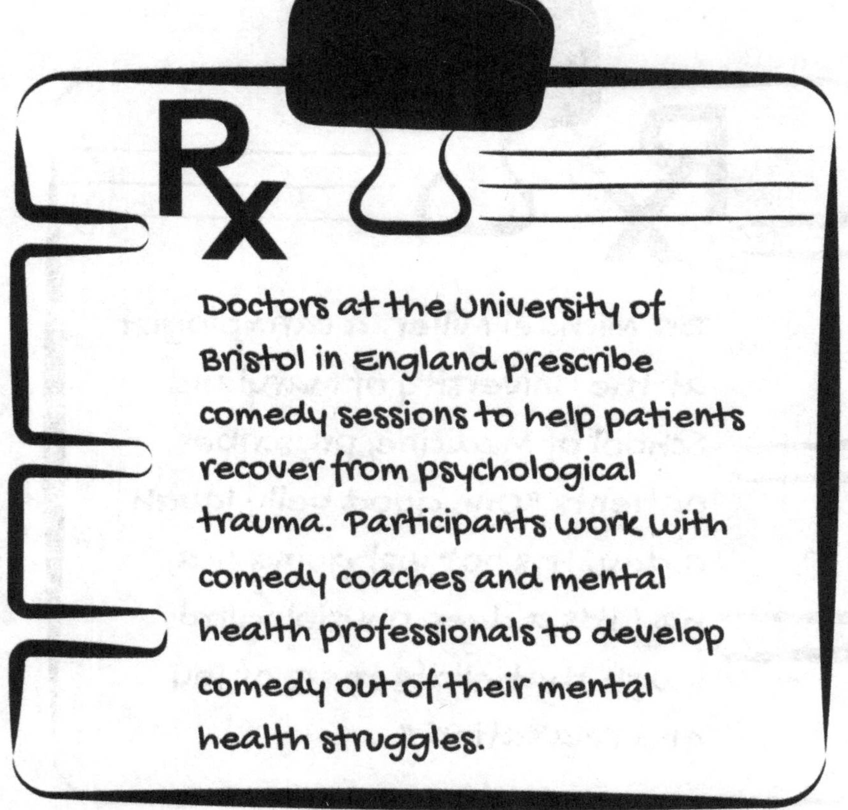

Rx
Doctors at the University of Bristol in England prescribe comedy sessions to help patients recover from psychological trauma. Participants work with comedy coaches and mental health professionals to develop comedy out of their mental health struggles.

FIGURE 2.3 R_x for stand-up comedy to cope with trauma. (Adapted from [30])

FIGURE 2.4 R_x for improv comedy to ease anxiety. (Adapted from [31,32])

And according to Dr. Frank Lipman, it's actually pretty close. He says that laughter "massages our internal organs."[33] I don't even know what that means, but it sounds great! I can't remember the last time I had an internal organ massage. "Ha, ha, ha, ha—oh, that feels good . . . I think that was my pancreas!" As one of the world's foremost humor and laughter researchers, Dr. Lee Berk put it:

"If we took what we now know about laughter and bottled it, it would require FDA approval."

Well, there you have it—a sampling of the research behind why humor helps our well-being. Simply put, it helps us increase our capacity to . . . "*even*." Also, it's just easier than mastering a yoga scorpion pose.

Laughing is easy. Scorpion pose is hard

I could go on with research about the *why* of humor, but I know you're here for the *how*. For all of you data-driven research enthusiasts, don't be sad. As I share specific humor habits and strategies, I'll sprinkle in some more data to show you why they work.

3 Improv(e) Your Mindset

If you relate with the dilemma of balancing your professional and playful side, or you suffer from a bit of stress and chronic seriousness, and all that data has you convinced that humor can help . . . now what? The first step is to get into a humor mindset. When it comes to getting out of your head, letting go, and learning not to take yourself so seriously, the principles of improv comedy provide a perfect framwork. If you aren't familiar with improv, here's a super brief overview:

- *Improv* is short for *improvisation*.
- There is no script or written jokes. Everything is made up in real time on the spot in front of the audience.
- The improv actors or "players" may take suggestions from the audience of a profession, place, relationship, activity, and so on, and use that to create a humorous scene.
- Some improv consists of "short-form" games where perhaps one character tries to guess who other characters are or it may consist of "long-form" scenes with deeper characters and plot lines.

Just like in real life, the goal with improv is to try to roll with the unexpected events that come our way to the best of our abilities, hoping for a positive outcome. As you can imagine, there's no time or room for improv actors to overthink things or worry about what others are thinking of them. They must be free to explore, play, and be a little weird. Here are some examples of the core tenets and strategies of improv, and how they might help you combat chronic seriousness in real life.

Be Present

In Improv:

Perhaps I have an idea of a great character I want to play in my next improv scene—a self-centered astronaut who doesn't care about the job but just wants to take selfies in the cool space outfit, next to the shuttle, and on the moon. It's kind of a funny premise, but if I'm busy planning this out in my head and not present in the moment, I'll screw up the scene. The audience suggestion might be a parent-teacher conference gone wrong and my scene partner begins assuming the role of a parent. What does that have to do with my preplanned astronaut?

Being present is about observing and being aware of what is happening in the moment. For example, in an improv scene I can't worry about the future of where I want things to go, try to recreate a funny scene from three nights ago, or worry about what the audience might be thinking at the time. I have to immerse myself in my character and in the moment.

In Real Life:

A college counselor once told me, "Thinking too much about the past is a recipe for depression and thinking too much about the future is a recipe for anxiety." This comment has stuck with me for 25 years. Even if it doesn't lead to depression or anxiety, thinking too much about the past or future prevents us from experiencing life in the moment. If you're in your head thinking about the agenda for tomorrow's staff meeting while taking your kids to the park, chances are you're going to miss the hilarious thing one kid said to the other. Similarly, there's a difference between mindlessly devouring an ice cream cone while ruminating over that conversation you had with a colleague last week versus savoring how good those little brownie chunks in the ice cream taste and smirking at the fact that it's getting all over your face.

When in doubt, look to kids and pets as your model. They have great lives with limited responsibilities, so they're experts at experiencing life in the moment. Watch how a toddler will sit and just run their hands through grass or sand, experiencing how it feels. A dog won't think twice about sticking its head out a car window to feel the breeze. To combat chronic seriousness, simply try to ground yourself with a sensation in the moment. What do you hear, see, feel, or smell? I have to practice this. When I take my dogs for a walk on a trail near my house, I'm often thinking about work-related things and going through my to-do list. When I begin to take in the smell of the trees and the sight of the narrow trail in the forest, I start feeling more like a kid out exploring in the woods. This is when I know I'm chipping away at the rigidity and seriousness of the day.

Listen. Like, *Really* Listen.

In Improv:

Because improv scenes are unscripted, it's crucial that the actors are intently listening to one another before determining what to say or do next. In the prior example of a "parent-teacher conference gone wrong" scene, my partner might say something like, "It's ridiculous that you gave Tommy a *D* on that paper because I . . . er, HE worked very hard on it." If I'm not listening closely, I could miss the subtle "I . . . er HE" moment, which sets up a hilarious premise for our scene—a parent who is offended at the kid's grade because they've been doing all the kid's homework for him.

In Real Life:

In both our personal and professional lives, people may open the door for humorous interactions, but we miss those invitations because we aren't really listening. This can be particularly common at work because many jobs require us to answer the same questions or have the same conversations with clients and customers multiple times per day, making it difficult to stay present and really listen. Take being a doctor as an example. One study found that patients initiate humor in a clinical setting at about the same rate as clinicians.[1] How great is that? There's the invitation for humor right there! The bad news, however, is that not all clinicians are present or listening to hear the invitation. In 67% of encounters after the clinician asks a patient how they're doing, they interrupt the patient in an average time of 11 seconds.[2] To be fair to doctors, I seriously doubt it's the only profession with a phenomenon like this. I assume this pattern exists in most industries where people have multiple similar conversations each day. Whether you're a bus driver, interior designer, financial planner, or attorney, chances are you have some human interactions and conversations that can feel repetitive.

While you will learn in future chapters, ways to develop your sense of humor so at some point you'll be the one initiating the humor, it doesn't always need to come from you. Simply listening for and noticing slightly humorous comments or laughter from others is a great start. Take, for example, Sarah, a clinical social worker who was meeting with a client talking about depression and suicide. Just after Sarah told her client, "I'm concerned that you've been thinking about suicide," they heard the deep sound of the timpani drums from a music therapy room down the hall with a dramatic "Bum bum, bum bum, bum bum!" The client let out a small chuckle at the sound of the drums. Because Sarah was present and listening, she was able to follow suit and laugh along with her. This spontaneous moment of humor led to the client opening up with Sarah more than she had before. Now, any time their conversations take a more serious tone, one of them will say, "Bum bum, bum bum, bum bum!"

Sometimes the best way to get out of a more serious head space is to listen to others and follow their lead. If they're using humor with you, then it probably makes them more comfortable. Just like in improv comedy, you listen for opportunities and then proceed with positive intentions.

Notice Gifts

In Improv:

A cool thing about improv is that there are no mistakes—only gifts. If I accidentally trip over a chair entering the stage, rather than panic, my scene partner will likely notice the gift and say something like, "Carl, you're the clumsiest surgeon I've ever worked with." Now they've gifted that right back to me—I can play off the fact that my character is a clumsy surgeon.

In Real Life:

There are plenty of real-world examples of peopling *improv*-ing their mindset by seeing mistakes as gifts:

The Mistake—In 1928, Alexander Fleming ruined an experiment when he left a petri dish on a lab bench instead of putting it away in an incubator. The bacteria in the petri dish were contaminated by a mold that prevented them from growing.

The Gift—That bacterium-preventing mold led to the development of the first antibiotic, penicillin.[3]

The Mistake—Kutol Products' soft, pliable compound meant for cleaning soot off wallpaper was deemed obsolete in the 1950s as homes transitioned to cleaner heating methods.

The Gift—One of the principal investor's sister-in-law, Kay Zufall, who was a nursery school teacher, let her kids make things with the nontoxic material. It was a hit, and she even thought of the name for the product, Play-Doh, that would eventually end up in the National Toy Hall of Fame in 1998.[4]

The Mistake—Over 40 years ago, scientist Spencer Silver was trying to create a "bigger, stronger, and tougher adhesive." He failed at this as the adhesive he made was only very light and tacky.

The Gift—If you can't figure out what the gift was from the wimpy adhesive, put a Post-it note on this page and come back to it.[5]

Reframing mistakes into gifts isn't easy and it takes practice, which is why many large organizations encourage employees to take risks and even fail. From rewarding employees who had massively failed ideas to hosting fail parties and a failed idea hall of fame, companies like Google, Coca-Cola, Netflix, Amazon, Intuit, and Domino's make risk-taking part of their culture.[6,7] They understand that, just like in improv comedy, it's difficult to be successful in business when people play it safe, are afraid to take risks, and make no mistakes.

Even if you're a NASA scientist working on *Apollo 13* and "Failure is Not an Option," you can still use this improv reframe at home in your everyday life. A prime example is Canadian neurosurgeon Dr. Eric Massicotte's viral Twitter (now X) post of a photo of his son's marker drawing on the living room wall. His wife, Kim, told me she caught their two boys in the act drawing on the wall in permanent marker. It was a hectic morning and she didn't see the humor in it immediately as she yelled, "Stop!" Several hours later, however, it occurred to her to have a little fun of her own. Rather than repainting the wall or trying to remove it, she put a frame around the drawing along with a label as though it were in an art gallery (Figure. 3.1). She posted a photo of their son's "gift" to the family on Dr. Massicotte's Twitter page and wrote "Your kids are going to do things they shouldn't. It helps if you married someone with a sense of humour."[8] Originally, Kim thought it would be a fun joke between the two of them, and had it been just that, it still would have been an excellent example of seeing a mistake as a gift and finding a little humor in it. However, the tweet garnered international news media attention, and resonated

Your kids are going to do things they shouldn't. It helps if you married someone with a sense of humor.

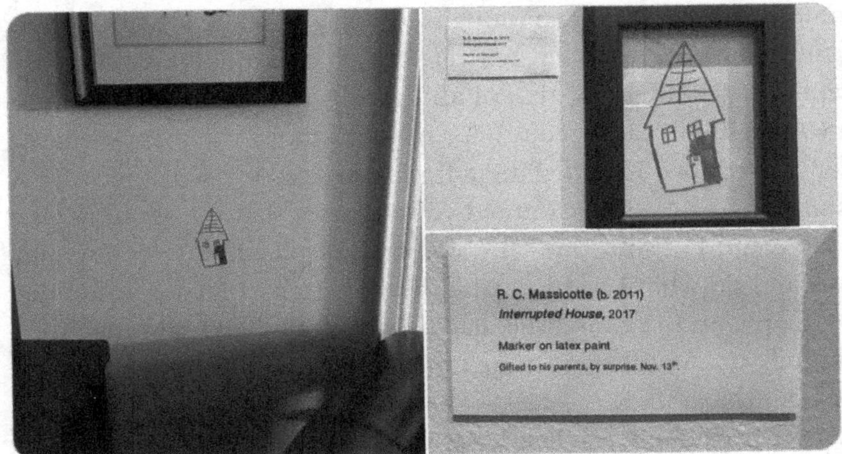

R. C. Massicotte (b. 2011)
Interrupted House, 2017
Marker on latex paint
Gifted to his parents, by surprise. Nov. 13th.

FIGURE 3.1 Twitter (now X) post of framed wall art. Turning their son's mistake into a gift.

with people all over the world. Six years later, the Massicottes still receive messages about how their light-hearted reaction to their son's mistake hit home for people. Dr. Massicotte told me "Yes, this mistake really can be seen as a gift and it's a gift that keeps on giving."

It's unrealistic to think our minds will immediately look at mistakes as gifts in the moment. Fortunately, unlike on an improv stage, we can have an initial moment of panic, freak-out, or stress before we figure out what the "gift" might be in a situation. That's normal. The Massicottes didn't see the permanent marker on the wall and immediately think "Wow, what an opportunity to be creative with our decorating and become an internet meme!" Making the drawing into a funny family art gallery was a thought that came later. And just like in improv comedy, the more you do it, the more often and quickly your mind notices the gifts.

One strategy to changing our mindset from mistakes to gifts is by changing our internal thoughts from, "Why is this happening *to me*?" to "How can I make this happen *for me*?" Years ago, I applied for a job as a career counselor at a community college. After sending in my application, I noticed an obvious typo on my résumé. I had my moment of panic and then thought of a way to make it work for me. At the end of the interview when asked if I had anything else to say, I replied, "Yes. I figured that of all the jobs to apply for with a typo on your résumé, career counselor may be among the worst—maybe after copyeditor." I handed them freshly printed revised copies of my résumé and said, "I just wanted you to know that if I get to be part of the team, I'm someone who will take responsibility for my mistakes and do what I can to make things better." I later learned that two people on the committee had seen the error and said they were definitely holding it against me until I did that in the interview. Oh, and I got the job!

Another example is when I was working at the university dealing with student disciplinary issues. I had a meeting with a student I had seen before for behavioral concerns. My first meeting with him was rough as he shot me dirty looks, got quite angry, and even yelled at me. This time he was in worse trouble and accompanied by his attorney and his mom. Just before going to the lobby to greet them, I spilled a 32-ounce cup of Dr. Pepper all over my lap. Without time to dry it or a find a clean pair of pants to change into, I knew the only way to go was to use it to break the ice. I went out to the lobby, called his name, looked down at my pants and said, "I hope your day is starting off better than mine." With a dry wit and the tiniest hint of a smile, he simply said, "I told you to see a doctor about that." His mom slapped his knee in shock, but his attorney, me, and the other five or six people in the office cracked up. As you would expect, our meeting this time went a lot better. This was truly a gift we gave to each other. I had nothing funny to say, but simply gave him the gift of my situation and a little humility. He then gave us all the gift of his funny reply, which served as an olive branch and amends for his behavior during our last encounter.

Say "Yes, and . . . "

In Improv:

Chances are you've heard of this rule of improv before, and for good reason. Saying "Yes and . . . " to the choices and actions your scene partner makes is crucial in improv. If I begin a scene saying, "Hurry, we've got to clear all these pigeons out of the plaza, fast!" and my partner says, "No, I'm not doing that" or "I don't see any pigeons," the scene goes nowhere, and we can't develop a story. However, if they accept my made-up premise and add to it, we can start to have some fun. Perhaps my partner says, "Right! We've got to clear the area so the town dance battle can begin!" Now we've got the making of a funny scene! The "Right!" is their "yes" and adding the ridiculous premise of a town dance battle in the plaza is their "and."

In Real Life:

A "Yes, and . . . " mentality in life is about trying to stay in a positive mindset and be open to possibilities. As serious adults, we learn to be logical, practical, and kind of boring, which results in us saying "Yeah, but," "What happens if . . . ?", "Not this time," or "No" a lot. There are a ton of opportunities to "Yes, and . . . " in life. If a friend asks if you'd like to go to Shakespeare in the Park and your first instinct is, "Yeah, but I'm too tired," try to muster a "Yes, and . . . I'm going to bring my goblet to drink wine out of!" Saying "yes" doesn't always mean agreeing to do something or that you agree with what is happening. It can also be about acknowledging the way things are in order build on top of it in a positive way. During the pandemic, many managers and leaders said "yes" simply by acknowledging that everything had to be virtual from now on. It didn't mean they liked it, but they started by acknowledging their new reality—just like in an improv scene. One leader of an organization I worked with did a great job of then saying "and" by having her team virtually show each other around their homes and introduce their families to one another. Essentially, this was saying "Yes, virtual meetings are our new reality, *and* let's see if we can have a little fun and get to know each other better." That simple exercise led to quite a bit of fun and humor for the group.

You're already keeping yourself open to possibilities and creating the right mindset by saying "yes" to reading this book. What will your "and" be?

Yes . . .

I'll read this book on humor and stress.

And . . .

I'll read it in a bubble bath every time.

or

I'll have a root beer float while I read it.

or

I'll complete all the activities at the end of each chapter.

By being present, really listening, noticing gifts, and having a "Yes, and . . . " mentality, you'll improv(e) your mindset and be ready to roll with anything that comes your way—even homework.

Humor Homework

Improv(e) Your Mindset

These lessons from improv comedy will help you begin to develop your humor mindset.

Be Present

This week, try some of these to keep yourself from going through the motions or getting stuck in mindless routines.

- Drive a different way to work or errands.
- Shop at a new grocery store.

- Reverse or change the order you do things (the order you dry off body parts after a shower, getting dressed, mowing the lawn, etc.).
- Reorganize your personal space occasionally (organize socks or shirts by color, then function, then favorites).
- Mix up the order of app icons on your phone.
- Write (perhaps even the following reflection) with your opposite dominant hand or do anything like hold a drink, use your phone, or use your mouse with your opposite hand.

Try these to keep your mind from wandering into the future or past:

- Take a deep breath and while holding it name five things you can see, feel, or hear.
- Play the A–Z game and go through the alphabet naming things you see around you, starting with *A*.
- Stop what you're doing, look around, and smile for no reason.

Doing things a new way or with a beginner's mindset not only helps us stay present, but increases the chances of noticing the absurd, interesting, fun, amusing, or fulfilling nuances of the everyday. What did you notice when trying some of the previous activities? Did you feel more present or aware? Did you feel silly or awkward? If so, that's a great step toward an improv(ed) mindset!

Listen. Like, REALLY Listen.

This week, in conversations with friends, family members, colleagues, and clients/customers try to focus on being a good listener. You already know some good listening habits:

- Put distractions like phones/computers away (even if it's off, take that one damn ear bud out of your ear).
- Try not to interrupt or shift the conversation back to your story.
- Be genuinely curious to learn more—ask clarifying questions.
- Face the person and give minimal encouragers like nods and "uh-huh's."
- Resist the urge to start talking—even if it's a bit awkward. I try to use a rule *"three and then me"*—I'll ask at least three clarifying questions and/or wait for three more seconds AFTER it feels like I should chime in.

What was it like to listen more intently? What did you notice? Did you notice any unexpected moments of levity or invitations for humor?

Notice Gifts

List five "mistakes, failures, or inconveniences" you've experienced that you can reframe as "gifts." You don't need to make them funny; we'll get to that later on.

Example

The Mistake: My wife, Kelly, and I were going cross-country skiing. I put the skis on our new roof rack and forgot to lock it down shut. As we were driving up the road two of them flew off and before we could get turned around to go get them, they were run over several times and damaged enough that we couldn't use them that day. To make it worse, it was one ski of each of ours that was damaged rather than just one pair.

The Gift: We told the staff at the small ski lodge what happened, and they let us use some gear for the day. The skis and bindings needed repair, but it only cost about $100, and we were extremely lucky there weren't any cars directly behind us when the skis flew off the roof. So the real gift is that the likelihood of me doing that again is extremely slim because I triple-check the roof rack every time. I was able to learn that lesson for under $100 and nobody getting hurt. Now every time we go skiing, we think of the amusing memory of me running up the road to grab the skis before they get pummeled again. Plus, the people who helped us out made us feel good about the new area and community we had moved to.

Your turn

1. *The Mistake:*
   The Gift:
2. *The Mistake:*
   The Gift:
3. *The Mistake:*
   The Gift:
4. *The Mistake:*
   The Gift:
5. *The Mistake:*
   The Gift:

Say "Yes, and . . ."

List five things you've said "no" to that you wish you hadn't. They could be big, like taking a new job out of state, or small, like having lunch with a friend the other day.

1.
2.
3.

4.
5.

Looking back on those, are there any themes? Are they similar opportunities? Did you say "no" for similar reasons like feeling too tired, overwhelmed, anxious?

List five things you've said "yes" to that brought you some joy or fulfillment. Again, this could be as big as going on a cruise with your sibling or as small as going to see your neighbor play live music on a work night.

1.
2.
3.
4.
5.

Looking back on those, were you initially hesitant to do any of them? If so, what made you decide to say "yes"? What was it about these experiences that brought you the most satisfaction? Did you add an "and" to any of these "yeses"? If not, how could you have?

This month, try to "Yes and . . . " at least once at home and once at work.

Home Example

Kid: Can I build a fort in the living room?

Typical Answer: Sure, honey.

Yes and . . . answer: Yes, and I'll help you make it the biggest one yet!

Work Example

Colleague: Looks like we'll all need to come in on Saturday to finish up this project

Typical Answer: I know, that sucks. See you then.

Yes and . . . Answer: Yes, and I'm bringing my 90s rock playlist and three boxes of Girl Scout cookies!

What did you "Yes, and . . ." this week? Did you notice any changes in your own attitude or behavior after? What about in others?

4 Cultivate and Consume

I was the closing keynote speaker for a tech leadership symposium, and in an audience of about 1,500 people, I could see that almost everyone was engaged, having fun, and laughing . . . except one dude. There's always that one guy sitting near the front with his arms folded looking like he'd rather be prepping for a colonoscopy. When I was finished, of course, the first person who came to speak to me was that dude. To my surprise, the first thing he said when he approached the stage was, "I liked your talk . . . . " Then he went on to share, "But I don't think I have a sense of humor. I think I forgot how to laugh." He went on to explain how his job in cyber security feels so heavy all the time, he feels very isolated from the rest of his colleagues, and he's had a lot of family health issues that have been adding to his stress. He added, "These days, it just doesn't seem like there's much to laugh about."

That's a fair statement. Human beings have never lived in an age where we're exposed to the amount of stress and trauma as we are now. Humans have existed on this planet for about 300,000 years and we've only had the internet for 30 and social media for half that. We're living in a weird social experiment where instead of just dealing with stressors from our immediate community, we're simultaneously exposed to the trauma of school shootings, wildfires, war, and other violence.

The reality, however, is that there's still just as much in the world to laugh about as there is to worry about. The problem is that our brains are hardwired with a negativity bias that causes us to consistently focus on what's wrong rather than what's right.[1] This was a great feature that helped our ancient ancestors stay alert for an incoming storm or an attacking pterodactyl. Now our brains use this feature for online doom scrolling or to point out others' mistakes—like the fact that humans didn't live in the Mesozoic Era with pterodactyls.

Being hyperaware of all the bad things and potential threats around us is great to help us survive, but it doesn't help us thrive. Therefore, we need to train our brain to see the funny and delightfully absurd things around us. It was clear the guy at my talk had been suffering from chronic seriousness for some time. It was also clear that although he admittedly used to have one, he had resigned himself to the thought that he's just someone without much of a sense of humor.

For some reason, a sense of humor is talked about like something we either have or lack—or perhaps we have a great one or a bad one. When someone is too serious all the time, we'll say, "Oh, he has no sense of humor." Conversely, you might have a fun, quick-witted friend who's always the life of the party—"She's got such a great sense of humor!" For someone like the guy at my talk, who's dealing with a lot, doesn't easily see the funny moments in life anymore, rarely thinks of funny things to say or do, and doesn't laugh as often as he used to, this dichotomy of either having or not having a sense of humor can be discouraging. The good news is that unless you're a complete sociopath, you have a sense of humor! It might just need a little workout.

I've had people tell me they like the thought of using humor more, but they're just not that talented. The fact is . . .

Humor is not a talent. **Humor is a habit.**

Any comedian, humorist, or humor writer will tell you the same. Humor is a mindset, a skill, a way of being, and a habit you can develop.

Using humor to cope with stress and overwhelm is no different than other well-being strategies in that it takes practice and consistency. If you started playing tennis, doing yoga, meditating, playing a musical instrument, or creating pottery to enhance your well-being, you wouldn't expect to be an expert at it right away. Although some people may have a natural proclivity to some of these activities, all of them—including humor—can be learned. The first step in this process is to immerse yourself in humor and begin to discover which types of humor captivate your mind, amuse your funny bone, or tickle your mustache. The humor habits in this chapter are about cultivating a collection, and then consuming humor. Think of it like learning a new language through immersion.

Follow Funny

The easiest thing to do is to start with social media. Let's face it, our computers and phones are really just mirrors. If I spend time online reading news articles or shopping for shoes, then my social media feeds will be all shoes and news! Maybe even some news about shoes, and who needs that? But we can use those techy algorithms to our advantage. You may just assume that if you use social media, there's a decent chance you'll come across something funny. Why leave it to chance? The first key to enhancing your sense of humor is to learn to **experience humor, not by chance, but by choice.** You're going to prime the pump for positivity.

Take a half an hour or so to funny up your feed. Like and follow people, shows, and pages you think are funny. If you love Stephen Colbert, then why aren't you following him on Instagram? Do you love memes? Search "memes" on Facebook and follow one of the pages dedicated to them. TikTok is an incredible humor hotbed, and their algorithm is great in terms of delivering you more of the content you watch, like, and comment on. So, if you're wondering why your version of TikTok is all makeup tutorials and home DIY videos, just look in the mirror (after you hang it on some studs and use it to put your makeup on, of course). Use the "saved" or "favorites" options in your social apps to hang on to and organize those videos that crack you up so you have easy access to them! Don't forget about YouTube. Search for your favorite comedians, talk show hosts, shows, or funny clips, and create a humor playlist that will be your go-to when you need a laugh.

There always will be new social media platforms to explore, and exploration is the key. Some people have asked me, "What if I don't know what kind of online humor I like?" That's okay! This is the time to cast a wide net and just watch, follow, and like various types of humorous content online. As you start clicking on more humor, the magic little tech elves that live in your device will keep offering more related things they think you might like. You may not like everything you come across, which is fine because over time your feed will become more and more refined due to the tech elves' algorithms. By the way . . . is it because Al Gore invented the internet that social media apps use Al Gore Rhythms? (I'm simultaneously both very proud and ashamed of that pun.) Anyway, nothing has to be permanent. If you started following your brother-in-law's sketch comedy group page because you felt obligated, you can always unfollow it or choose not to see posts anymore . . . he'll never know.

Crowdsourcing is an excellent way to get exposed to more humor. In a post, tell your friends and online connections, "I'm in search of some good humor. Who should I follow, what pages should I like, and what movies/TV shows do you recommend?" Trust me, everyone wants to be the first one to tell you about that new show they're bingeing or put you on to that hilarious Instagram account they found. You don't just have to crowdsource for social media–related humor either. Ask about funny books, memoirs, magazines, local comedy shows, and so on.

Have a Humor Homie

Another way to curate your comedy collection is to find a "Humor Homie." This is just a friend whom you'll make an agreement to send each other one funny thing each day without the obligation of any comments or replies. You don't need to respond with a "Oh, yeah, I've seen that" or "LOL, that hat though!" unless you want to. It can be a photo, meme, video, podcast episode, or anything you find funny. The point is to have someone you're accountable to for finding and sending one humorous thing each day. This will get you in the habit of looking for humor and it will help you build your collection since you'll find one funny thing and receive one funny thing each day. The cool thing is that even if you don't have time to watch that video your friend sent yet, and you need to wait until your lunch break or when you get home—just the *anticipation* of that humor can lead to a 39% decrease in stress.[2] So, if you've read this far in the book and haven't found one thing funny yet, but you're just waiting on the edge of your seat anticipating that I might be funny once . . . at least your stress levels are decreasing.

Take a "Funny 15"

We know that people who take a 15-minute break at work are more productive when they get back to work (duh), but according to the *Journal of Business Psychology*, people who watched a funny video on their break were twice as productive when they returned as those who took a break with no humor![3] Set an alarm to take a break to watch a couple of the funny videos you've collected. Not only will this keep your brain in humor-immersion training, it will also keep you sharper and more productive for the rest of the day.

A humor break is particularly effective if you've just experienced a stressful meeting or situation in your day as laughter can moderate stress symptoms after stressful events. Specifically, the more frequently you laugh around the time a stressful event occurs, the fewer and weaker the stress symptoms you're likely to have related to that event.[4] Because you've started curating a comedy collection with your social media accounts, it works out that you've got humor at the ready to combat life's drama with comedy. Of course, if you're like me you may need to set another alarm at the end of your break to stop watching funny stuff and get back to work. If your boss asks why you're watching videos of cats falling into fish tanks at work, just stand up straight, put a pencil behind your ear, raise one eyebrow, and hit 'em with, "I'm optimizing my productivity for this afternoon. Humor has been found to be one factor that can mitigate and counteract the effects of mental depletion."[5]

Screening Your Screen Time

Although it's fun and super convenient to experience humor via movies, TV, and social media videos, practice responsible adulting by being mindful about mindless bingeing. It turns out our brains can get fairly addicted to the dopamine those little screens provide. Here are a few ways to be dopamine-diligent with your screen time:

- **Comedy Chaser:** Even if you get really into the first few humor habits, chances are you'll still be consuming a fair share of more serious media. Whether it's cable news, action movies, dramas, or a true crime serial killer documentary (why are those so popular right now?), the intensity and stress from that type of media can linger. Rather than take that with you to bed or to work, consider a funny palette cleanser. Even if it's only a couple of minutes, make the final thing you watch on a screen something funny. With a comedy chaser, the final thing you watch for the day will be stress-*reducing* and not stress-*inducing*.
- **Play it by ear:** Podcasts are a terrific way to find some funny. Rather than watching a late-night talk show host's monologue or your favorite stand-up special, many of them have podcast versions. Not to mention, comedians and comedic actors are producing their own podcasts at near Silicon Valley tech-bro levels. I used to listen to news podcasts or work-related audio books

on my work commute and realized it was adding to my anxiety and stress. Now that I think about it—duh. On my way to spend the next eight hours helping students in distress, I'm probably not boosting my energy and increasing my capacity to deal with stress by listening to a podcast on "Why Today's Generation of Students Is More Depressed than Ever." I noticed that when I listened to news or work-related podcasts, I would already feel tense before even arriving at work. Give some thought about what's playing in those earbuds and how it's affecting you. Do a search for the top funny podcasts of the year or, again, crowd-source ideas from friends.

- **Turn the page**: Don't forget about getting away from the screen by indulging in the old-school book or magazine—and your reading list doesn't always have to look like it was curated by TED Talks. Conversations about what transformative and foundational business or personal development book you're reading have become part of the chronically serious culture we live in. Along with Brené Brown, Steven Covey, and Simon Sinek, be sure to throw in a memoir from Tina Fey, Sarah Cooper, Seth Rogen, or Mindy Kaling. Next time you're at the store, treat yourself to a fun magazine. It doesn't have to be funny or humorous, just light-hearted and something you enjoy, like cooking, fishing, golf, art, or crosswords.
- **Go Live**: Just like music, the absolute best way to experience comedy is live and in-person. Google live comedy in your area and check out some stand-up, improv, sketch, or musical comedy. If you don't have a professional comedy club in town, chances are there's a high school or college performance or an occasional open mic somewhere nearby. Also, just like music, comedy is a subjective art form. The first show you go to may or may not be your humor jam, but don't let that stop you from checking out a different show another time.

Learn to Laugh

"We don't stop laughing because we get old.
We get old because we stop laughing."

—George Bernard Shaw

Now that you've curated a comedy collection, you've got some stuff to laugh at. While you don't *have* to laugh to reap the benefits of humor, laughter will turbocharge those effects. You've already learned about how good laughter is for you, and the unfortunate truth that we laugh far less often after the age of . . . remember? If you said 23, congratulations on your brain's ability to retain random facts! You should be on a trivia team.

As a comedian, you'd think I would laugh a lot. I do now, but several years ago I realized that I just didn't laugh very often. I wasn't as chronically serious as the guy who told me he "forgot how to laugh" after my talk, but I just wasn't laughing much even when I was having a good time. I have a friend who has such a great laugh. He laughs all the time and I had always been kind of jealous of that. I wanted to be that guy! When I would watch fellow comedians, I would intellectualize everything and be thinking so much that even if I thought it was funny, I wouldn't laugh. It was like I was devouring a piece of pie over a garbage can before running to a meeting. Yeah, it was good, but did I really let myself enjoy it? The same would happen when I watched movies. Do you ever do that? Watch a video or movie and you genuinely do think it's funny, but instead of really laughing you kind of grin a little or even just matter-of-factly say, "That's hilarious." I found myself doing that a lot and I wanted to be someone who laughs more often and more deeply. Believe it or not, I was actually able to change that! And you can too. Here are a few ways to get yourself to really laugh.

- **Be humor positive:** This means being open-minded and receptive to the humor you're about to partake in. As a comic, I noticed there were two types of audience members. Those who were generous with their laugh and those who withheld it.

When your laughter threshold is set too high.

In fact, I used to be the latter. Back when I wasn't laughing much, I used to watch movies, shows, and live comedy with the mindset that "this better make me laugh." If a brain could have its arms folded, that's how mine was.

When I switched my mindset to "I can't wait to laugh," things changed. Essentially, I had my laughter threshold set too high and there was no reason to withhold it. We don't need to conserve our laughs like they'll run out someday. In fact, the more we use them, the more they generate. One simple way to start that mindset shift is to begin with a smile on your face. Let's practice. Whether you're at your office, or in your car, I want you to just put the shape of a smile on your face. You don't have to mean it. You can be thinking, "How long do I have to do this?" or "How will he know if I'm really doing it?" or anything else. If you can't even muster a fake smile, you might be suffering from erect-smile dysfunction, and you'll have to ask your doctor about that. Just by putting the shape of a smile on your face (whether you mean it or not), you're able to trick your brain into being in a more emotionally positive state.[6] This will help you relax and access your sense of humor. Being humor positive will help lower your laughter threshold and help you stay open to new types of humor.

- **Kick it up a notch and fake it 'til you make it:** This might sound strange, but I started to simply exaggerate (just a little) my own reaction to humor. If something made me smile, I would let out a little "*heh.*" If something gave me two little chuckles, I would purposely make them a little louder and longer. If something made me laugh, which I used to do quietly, I tried to let myself go, and just do it a little deeper and longer than I typically would have. It felt weird at first, but I began to notice a difference quickly! Not only would I feel more relaxed, but I was way more likely to laugh again later, and before I knew it, it didn't feel like I was forcing it at all. Now, I can honestly say that I genuinely laugh multiple times every day at something—whether it's a TikTok video, or my dog getting stuck in a blanket. The best part is, I actually like my laugh too! It's a deep belly laugh mixed with an occasional wheeze. I'm that guy now!
- **Laugh at nothing:** Finally, if you really want to get some health benefits of laughter then try some "laughter yoga" or doing a "laughie," which is like a selfie video of you laughing. These are essentially deep-breathing exercises in the form of voluntary laughter. I know, it sounds kind of crazy, but the research is incredible. Studies found that 70% of people who took a one-minute video of themselves laughing and then watched and laughed along with it increased both their immediate and overall World Health Organization well-being scores.[7] The best part is that most participants found their own laughter contagious. If you want to make it a group activity, there are laughter yoga groups that meet in person or online that take participants through various laughter exercises.

Allowing ourselves to laugh more deeply and more often helps us psychologically because we're actually feeling emotions. We're learning to access that childlike feeling of laughter that for whatever reason, we've learned to bottle up at times. So, as you consume the humor you've collected from the previous habits, put a smile on your face before you start and say to yourself, "I can't wait to laugh."

Humor Homework

Cultivate and Consume

Internet with Intention

To perform the humor habits in this chapter, you may need to spend some time exploring or rediscovering what type of humor you're into. Remember, your little handheld robot computer is pretty smart, so if you loved the TV show *Friends* and search for it, you'll get other suggestions for similar comedy. Try not only searching for specific comedians or shows, but broader searches like "best 90s stand-up comedy" or "funniest sketch comedy." For more specific ideas and categories of humor and comedy to search for online, check out the "Types of Comedy and Humor" list in the supplement materials at TheHumorHabit.com.

Humor Habits

Choose as many of the Humor Habits from this chapter to complete and write about how they went. If you complete more than three, then raise one eyebrow and say, "I am quite impressive, aren't I?" in a British accent. (If you already have a British accent, go with French.)

- **Follow funny**—Optimize your social media channels by liking and following funny people and pages.
- **Have a humor homie**—Find a friend to share something funny with every day for a week.

- **Take a Funny 15**—Set an alarm to remind you to watch humorous videos during a work break.
- **Comedy Chaser**—Be sure the last media you consume for the day is humor.
- **Play it by ear**—Check out a new funny podcast.
- **Turn the page**—Substitute your "professional" reading for something fun or funny.
- **Go live**—Attend a live stand-up comedy performance, musical, play, or improv.
- **Learn to laugh**—Be humor positive, kick it up a notch, or laugh at nothing.

Which humor habits did you choose? What differences have you noticed? Feel free to come back to this prompt after trying new ones!

5 Develop a Funny Focus

> "I don't go, 'I'm gonna write a joke.' I just go through the world and see stuff. It's like I exercise the part of my mind of noticing things, to the point where I'm now noticing things without even trying to notice them."
>
> —Comedian Steven Wright

Early in my speaking career I was selected to give a TED-Talk–style presentation at a massive marketing conference in Boston. There were more than 20,000 attendees and some of the featured speakers included Issa Rae, Brené Brown, Adam Grant, and Michelle Obama. This was an incredible opportunity for me to get my name out there and connect with leaders from major brands and Fortune 500 companies. Needless to say, I went into full chronic seriousness "cool guy networking" mode. At the end of every conversation, I would immediately dig into the breast pocket of my blazer, grab my business card, and say something like, "Well hopefully we can work together sometime" or "I'd love to stay connected." I was hitting people with business cards like a Macy's beauty consultant with free samples of Chanel No. 5. At the height of me taking myself a little too serious and covering everyone in my own "Eau de Desperation," I found myself talking with an executive of a large company.

At the end of our conversation, as he was about to walk away, I awkwardly fumbled in my pocket for a business card like a dolphin grabbing a bar of soap. Then I blurted, "Wait! Give me a call sometime," as I handed him my . . . hotel room key. He looked at it strangely and with a straight face replied, "Well that escalated quickly." My neck and face turned red as I sheepishly mumbled, "Oh, sorry, hehe. I meant to give you this."

It's so easy to look back on that moment now and see how funny it was. In fact, I use this story on stage sometimes and it always gets a laugh. The weird thing, though, is that in the moment, I didn't see the humor in it. I was devastated and embarrassed. I could have easily just laughed with him, or met his comment with a "Yes, and . . . " For example:

Executive: "Well that escalated quickly."
Me: "Right!? And I snore, so bring some earplugs!"

But I didn't do that. I let chronic seriousness take over, handed him the card, and replayed the awkward encounter in my head for the next hour. I was so focused on getting leads, being taken seriously, and capitalizing on the opportunity this event provided that my brain was processing my life as though it were a drama.

It wasn't until a couple of days later when telling the story to someone else that I was able to see it as a scene in a comedy. I made something so silly become such a big deal. In fact, because of the funny mistake, it was probably a much more memorable interaction for the executive I was speaking with than if it had been a perfectly executed "professional" networking interaction. Now, here we are eight years later and that executive and I . . . have never spoken again. It's not a Disney movie, okay. I totally flubbed it. Sometimes you just screw stuff up and it's awkward and funny, and not the end of the world.

I wish I didn't get so flustered in that moment and let it stress me out. I wish I could have seen the humor in real time. In the last chapter, we focused on intentionally collecting and consuming humor

My brain turning my life from a comedy into a drama.

that others have created to counteract your brain's negativity bias. The next step is to develop your sense of humor to the point that your brain can recognize or create humor from the scenes of *your* life. Why did I get so stressed and embarrassed during that interaction with the executive, and what would have happened if I saw the humor in real time? I'll never know because my brain just didn't think that way in the moment. The good news is that because of the neuroplasticity of our brains (I just wanted to say *neuroplasticity* to sound super smart), we're able to create new thinking patterns and habits so we can actually train our brains to have more of a "funny focus" and see the humor in life more often. This is called the priming effect[1]—our brains are wired to see what we're set up to expect.

We find what we choose to look for. Check this out—fill in the blank letter to complete the last word for each of these two lists:

Camping / Tent / Attack / Be _ r

Party / Keg / Chug / Be _ r

You went from being attacked by a bear to chugging a beer pretty quickly! We can train our brain by priming it to look for certain things. It's like when you decide to buy a new car you begin to see that car everywhere. Humor is everywhere as well. You just need to train your brain to see it more often, which is exactly what the habits in this chapter are designed to do. Now that you're already collecting and consuming humor, the exercises in this chapter will help you notice the humor around you and develop your own "funny focus."

Three Funny Things Intervention

The first habit is something I call the "Three Funny Things" intervention and it's a one-week challenge. For one week, simply write down three things each day that you found humorous, amusing, or funny. Maybe it made you laugh, maybe it just made you smile, or maybe you even just thought "that's kind of funny." Researchers have found that people who did this "Three Funny Things" intervention for just one week actually reduced depressive symptoms and increased overall happiness for up to six months![2] Not to mention the fact that positive psychology researchers are (predictably) super positive about the mental health benefits of journaling.[3] (Imagine researching positive psychology and happiness for a living. The pressure to always be in a good mood must be intense! If they can't figure out how to be happy, then how the hell are rest of us supposed to?)

The three things you think of at the end of the day could be something your kids or pets did, a joke someone told you, or an awkward Zoom meeting moment. It can even be stuff you didn't think was funny in the moment, but later in the day you see the humor in it. The great thing about this habit is, for one, it helps you remember the funny things that happen throughout your week. How often do you try to tell someone a story or joke and it's hard to remember exactly what made it so funny? By doing this one-week challenge, you will have collected 21 funny anecdotes or stories to remember. The other thing is that you're rewiring the neurons in your brain to begin firing when you see humor around you. Inevitably, what will happen when you do this exercise is that there will be something during your day that is mildly frustrating or stressful and you may roll your eyes and think to yourself, "Ugh, I'll be writing this one down tonight"—and that's when you know you're actually starting to see the humor in life in real time and not in retrospect. It isn't funny and didn't make you laugh . . . yet. But your brain is acknowledging that there's probably humor in the situation somewhere, which is enough to give you a little perspective in the moment and not feel as much uncontrollable stress or anxiety about it.

Humor Jar

Another strategy our happy positive psychology research friends encourage is savoring. I always used to think of savoring in terms of food—like savoring a juicy cheeseburger so much that you eat the cheese off the wrapper. And while a glob of greasy wrapper cheese is a euphoric part of the human experience, apparently there are more cholesterol-friendly methods of savoring. In his book on the topic, Dr. Fred Bryant explains that savoring can be done in the past, present, or future. We can increase our well-being by savoring the joys of everyday life as they happen, we can anticipate the exciting moments that are to come, or we can reminisce on past happy moments.[4] Specifically, reminiscing about past positive memories diminishes acute stress.[5] This humor habit will help you savor the present moment and provide you an opportunity to reminisce.

It's simple. Just find a glass jar or container and cut some strips of multicolored paper. Well, technically it doesn't have to be multicolored. If you're a minimalist, you can do this with a black box and white paper if that's your thing, or you can go to the craft store and go all Martha Stewart on it. My wife, Kelly, and I found a ceramic jar with words from an iconic Christopher Walken *Saturday Night Live* sketch stamped into it. Our humor jar sits in our kitchen and says: "More Cowbell" so, you do you. Have the jar, strips of paper, and a pen in an easily accessible place at home or in the office, and whenever a funny moment happens, write it down and put it in the jar. Then, at the end of the year, quarter, or month, depending on how many you have and how many people are participating, you can open the jar and relive all your funniest moments!

This humor habit is longer term and it's great for capturing those random, spontaneous, "you had to be there" funny moments from the day. What I like best about this activity is that it can involve as many people as you like. If the entire family or your whole office team has access to the jar, you'll end up with a ton of funny anecdotes to look back on. You'll also now be surrounded by people who have no idea they're rewiring their brains to savor funny moments when they happen and reminisce about previous positive experiences. They'll be decreasing their stress, causing them to freak out less, resulting in you having to respond to less drama, thus decreasing your stress. It's like a Jedi mind trick that benefits everyone. (By the way, do you capitalize Jedi? I'm just not sure if I treat it as a fictional job like wizard or a fictional race of people like Oompa Loompa.)

If you have kids and want to elicit their participation, a good way to start is to change up what you ask them about their day. Instead of "how was school"—which you already know the answer . . . "okay" or "fine." Ask them, what was something funny that happened at school today? And then encourage them to add it to the jar! If you ask them this consistently, they'll start going through their day looking for the humor to report back!

What's cool about the humor jar is you can save your favorite slips of paper to put in a funny file so you'll never forget! I still remember one of my favorites from the first year I did a humor jar. I was the

8 a.m. opening keynote speaker for a conference at a hotel. That morning I thought I would go downstairs and grab a tray of breakfast from the buffet in the lobby and take it up to my room to eat as I got ready. I hastily just threw on the clothes I was wearing the day before to sneak down and grab my food. When I got down there, the lobby was packed with conference attendees, so I was in line with others grabbing eggs, potatoes, and coffee. Then I noticed something. Every step I took, there was something creeping its way down the inside of my pant leg. It started mid-thigh, then went down to my knee and began slipping further. I froze when I realized . . . "Oh, no! Those are the underwear I was wearing yesterday that were still in my pants!" Now I'm standing there with a tray of food in my hands and one leg bent at the knee like a dirty, lazy, flamingo. I had to hobble my way back to the elevator without letting my underwear come out the bottom of my pant leg. It was embarrassing, but made for the perfect humor jar entry and something I don't think I'll ever forget.

Mirthful Mantra

Okay, I've got to admit that I've always been too skeptical and cynical to be a "calming mantra" guy. Yes, reciting mantras (which means "mind release" in Sanskrit), is shown to decrease stress, lower anxiety, and increase positive outlook,[6] but I always thought it also increased my chances of looking like a freak. If I'm sitting at my desk with my eyes closed repeatedly whispering "I am not angry, I am calm," it means I'm about to put a 7 iron through my monitor, eat an ink cartridge, and make snow angels on the carpet. Don't get me wrong, if you can do deep, serious, and earnest mantras to help you relax and refocus, you should. They work. And, while I can be an unsophisticated jack-wagon, even I'm able to have calm, introspective moments during the day to set my intentions. My issue has always been when stress or anxiety starts to build, I just can't take myself seriously saying, "I am exactly where I'm supposed to be" or "I am enough." So I figured mantras just weren't my thing.

Then, one day, I realized I do have a mantra! Mine just happened to come from a Bud Light commercial. There was a series of Bud Light commercials where peasants would try to impress a medieval king by bringing him fancy microbrew beer and mead wines. Of course, the king would only be impressed by Bud Light, and when he would receive some, he would delightfully shout "Dilly Dilly!" When people would bring the wrong gifts, he would send them to the pit of misery and everyone in the castle would shout "To the pit of misery! Dilly Dilly!" It didn't take long until I began shouting **"Dilly Dilly!"** when just about anything was going wrong.

> *"My boss told me we don't have the money to hire for the new assistant director position, so I'll assume those duties as well . . .* ***"Dilly Dilly!"***
>
> *"My sprinkler system sprung a leak the day I'm supposed to leave town . . .* ***"Dilly Dilly!"***
>
> *My rental car was broken into and my suitcase stolen right outside a police station while I was inside delivering a workshop for the officers . . .* ***"To the pit of misery! Dilly Dilly!"***

For some reason, this "Dilly Dilly!" phrase is just funny to me, and when things are bad, saying it to myself is somehow therapeutic. It made me realize that this too shall pass, which—gulp—is actually one of those serious mantras. I was "Dilly Dilly-ing" my way through things enough that my wife Kelly bought me a cool "Dilly Dilly!" engraved money clip for Christmas, which is in my pocket right now.

You might be thinking "Cool story, bro. Glad you got Bud en-Light-ened. But what does this have to do with me?" First, if you were thinking that, then great play on words with the "Bud en-Light-ened!" That deserves a round of drinks of your choice! The point is, your mantra doesn't have to be meditative. It can be anything that helps you refocus, put things in perspective, laugh it off, or ground yourself. Once I realized that mantras don't always have to be profound prose for Instagram stories and yoga studio walls, it became much easier for me. As a comedian and speaker, one of the most helpful mantras I tell myself when shit hits the fan is "It's all material." This helps me remember that most of my best stories and jokes come from the times when things go wrong or when I've done something idiotic.

Four Ways to Find Your Own Mirthful Mantra:

—**Movie Mantras**: Try to think less austere and powerful, and more Austin Powers. Think of a movie or TV show quote you love that will get you laughing or change your mindset. Perhaps it's Dr. Evil saying "Throw me a frickin' bone here." Or Ted Lasso's "Be a Goldfish" (because they only have 10-second memories).

—**Sarcastic Singing**: Take a moment to sing the most ridiculously upbeat or happy song lyric you know ironically or sarcastically. I do this a lot with a famous song from *The Lego Movie*. There's nothing like sarcastically singing "Everything Is Awesome!!!" while cleaning dog diarrhea off the carpet. Other songs in this genre include "Happy" by Ferrel and "Good Life" by One Republic.

—**Inside Jokes**: My "Dilly Dilly" mantra went from a commercial to an inside joke with me and Kelly to a therapeutic mind release. Perhaps you have inside jokes with your family or friends that will help you maintain perspective or put a smile on your face when you just can't even.

—**Serious Mantra Voiceover**: Maybe there's a more profound mantra that you like, but you're not sure you can take yourself seriously enough to do the deep breathing and repeating, or you just want to have some fun with it. Take your serious mantra and say it either in your head or out loud in a funny voice. For example, "This too shall pass" as Gandolf from *Lord of the Rings* or "I have a choice, and I choose peace" as Elmo.

Remember, as you try this out, don't stress about finding the perfectly witty mantra that will be "your thing" forever. It's easy (especially when we're stressed) to get paralyzed by permanence, even with small decisions or silly things like this. You may stumble across the perfect mantra someday, but the great thing about the stuff in this book is that it's all for you! You're an adult. You're not being graded on this and there will be no evaluation affecting salary decisions. Just have fun with it. Try one and if it doesn't work or you don't like it, you can always try something different!

You can also feel free to let others in on the joke if you want. Of course, your mantra can be something you only say to yourself in your head, but it doesn't have to be. We use "Dilly Dilly!" and "Everything is awesome!" at home, but "It's all material" is something I just say to myself. When I was working with college students with substance abuse and mental health challenges, sometimes our meetings with them and their parents would be intense and very stressful. One day after my final meeting of a day packed full of sad and emotionally exhausting cases, a student angrily walked out of our office with their parents and attorney shouting, "I HATE THIS F*****G SCHOOL!" As I passed my colleague in the back office she asked, "How are you doing?" and I defeatedly replied with a heavy sigh and said, "Oh, you know . . . changing lives." We both kind of chuckled, but from then on "Changing Lives" became a mantra and somewhat of a motivating battle cry in our office. We'd share a quick "Changing Lives!" with one another at times when things were stressful and hectic as well as when we had breakthroughs and moments to celebrate.

A nurse at a hospital I worked with shared that on one busy night as she was running from room to room, one of her sweet elderly patients grabbed her arm and in a very twangy southern accent said, "Breathe, Baayyby, breathe," and when she told her department teammates about it, it made them all smile. Now, of course, when things get overwhelming, they look at each other and in their best southern accents say, "Breathe, Baayyby, breathe!" It's amazing how quickly these funny mantras can catch on in a small group, and the power they can have to temporarily ground us, break through the acute stress wall we've built up, and give us the needed perspective to get through the moment.

From Seeing Funny to Being Funny . . .

The Three Funny Things Intervention, Humor Jar, and Mirthful Mantra are all about developing your funny focus by training your brain to see the funny things in life around you. They help you take notice of and savor the humor in life while giving you perspective that stressful things may not be as bad as they seem, and are perhaps, even funny at times. Rather than simply recognizing the humor that has already happened, with these habits, you'll need to work to find the funny.

For most people, going from seeing funny to being funny is difficult at first. Think of it like a flat six-pack stomach. I can notice and appreciate one when I see it, and I suppose everyone has one deep down there somewhere, but producing my own is going to be a lot harder than appreciating someone else's. That doesn't mean the consistent practice and exercise that's required to get to it isn't good for my body, even if there may always be people with stronger, and tighter jokes, er . . . abs.

In a study out of the University of Southern California, researchers monitored the brain scans of participants while they attempted to write funny captions to cartoons. There was a control group with no comedy experience, amateur comedians, and professional comedians. What they found was that the more experience people have using humor, the more they will shift from relying on the prefrontal cortex executive functioning part of their brains to guide searches for humorous associations to relying on the temporal lobe, which facilitates spontaneous and remote or abstract associations.[7] This means that the more we practice looking for humor and playing with the absurdities in life, the easier and more natural it comes to us. It also means that doing so gets us out of the list writing, meal planning, desk organizing, agenda preparing part of our brain and into the part that is more responsible for processing our emotions.

Long story short—with these next few humor habits, don't worry if they're hard at first or if what you come up with isn't hilarious. The exercise is good for you even if you don't see your six-pack abs right away.

Humorous Reappraisal

One of my favorite parts of traveling around and speaking about humor is getting to chat with people after my talks. Imagine getting a room full of people you've just met to come geek out with you about whatever your favorite obsession is. Some people love a particular sport, others are freaks about *Star Wars*, and I'm a proud Humor Nerd. So when a room full of physicians, financial advisors, or HR managers want to come talk nerdy to me about humor, I'm in humor heaven! (Which, by the way "humor heaven" is just like "regular heaven," except everyone is hilarious . . . but never as funny as you.) Anyway, one common theme from these post-keynote conversations is that regardless of demographic or industry, most people say they don't think of fun or funny ways to handle annoying or stressful situations in the moment. I get a lot of people who tell me, "Later on, I always think oh I should have said this, or I could have done that! That would have been funny." If that's you, then this Humor Habit is for you!

Psychologists at Stanford University conducted a study in which people are shown horrifying images and then asked to reappraise them in a more positive way, finding that the most effective form of cognitive reappraisal was when they used humor.[8] Participants had more increases in positive emotions and decreases in negative emotions when making any kind of funny quip, essentially reframing the situation in a humorous way. This is consistent with an array of research showing that humor helps people cope more successfully with traumatic situations and leads to greater positive affect and psychological well-being.[9]

Although Humorous Reappraisal is a much more professional and academic sounding name for this humor habit, I usually just call it the "What I Could've Said Game." When thinking about a negative or stressful situation from the past, you simply try to come up with alternative funny ways you could have handled it. It could be something from 10 years ago or from yesterday. While this humor habit works with heavy and even traumatic events, try starting with something small that's just mildly stressful or annoying. For example, maybe you're in an important meeting with all the company's top leaders and you bravely chime in to offer an incredible idea that is sure to impress the boss, but when gesturing you spill your 20-ounce coffee all over the place. You start apologizing profusely, turn a little red, and grab some towels to clean it up, but you never got to make your point because of how flustered and embarrassed you got. Later that night you think, "I wish I could have handled that with a little more levity. At least said or done something to play it off or get back on track." Cool, go with it! Play the game. What would you have said or done to add a little humor to the situation? Maybe after you spill, you could have said one of the following:

"Now that I have your attention . . . "

"Let's let this idea percolate for a minute . . . "

"This idea has already generated a latte excitement!"

"It's okay, it's just half & half. Half on the table . . . half in my lap"

Can you come up with one? Write it here!

____

Remember in Chapter 3 when I talked about how mistakes could be gifts? The mistake example I gave was when I forgot to latch down the ski rack on the car and one ski from each of my and my wife's pairs of cross-country skis slid off the roof of the car, into the road, and got ran over as we were driving up the hill. I was so pissed off and embarrassed, especially because we were going Nordic skiing with new friends. I didn't have any great funny thoughts in the moment, but what could I have said?

"Looks like they also work for downhill."

"Can you slalom?"

"Maybe instead of new skis I should have just bought brewskis."

You got one? ____________________

Your ideas of funny things you could have done or said don't have to be hilarious or make you laugh out loud—especially as you first try it. The goal is just to let your brain play with the premise of reacting with a little more levity. The more you play the game, the better you'll get at it, and the funnier your responses will get.

The cool thing about this technique is, just like the other humor habits, you're rewiring your brain to make humorous associations. You might play the "What I Could've Said Game" a day later, but the next time something happens you'll think about what to do a few hours later, then a few minutes later, and pretty soon you're making humorous associations in the moment. And even if the situation is too serious to find humor in the moment, looking back at past stressful events and using humorous reappraisal can be a way to reframe a memory from being traumatic or negative into more neutral or even positive.

A colleague of mine, Dr. Steve Sultanoff, is a psychotherapist and fellow Certified Humor Professional who uses humorous interventions in his sessions with clients. He shares an example of a client of his who was working through some anger issues. The man shared that he was ruminating over an incident where he was leaving a hair salon with his baby when someone said, "It's raining out there, don't let that baby get wet." The comment made the guy feel like the stylist was judging him and didn't think he knew how to be a parent. Dr. Sultanoff had him brainstorm funny things he could have said instead of getting mad. The client came up with: "It's okay, he hasn't had a bath in weeks" and "It's okay, I sprayed him with waterproofing before we left." This technique gives us some control over how we feel when remembering past stressors and makes it more likely that we'll roll with future stressors with a little more levity.

The point is, even if you're not great at laughing things off in the moment or saying and doing something to lighten the mood with humor spontaneously, it can be beneficial to your psychological well-being to do so after the fact. All too often we get consumed with stressful and negative thoughts about things that happened throughout the day or the week. We might ruminate on those negative experiences on our own or vent to our friends about it. If you're going to spend time and energy thinking about these stressful stories, why not see if you can change the genre of the story from a drama to a comedy?

Guess the Punchline

This habit is fun because it feels like a game, and you can play by yourself or with friends and family in the room. It's also a great way to exercise your humor muscle while still practicing some of the habits from Chapter 4 as you simply enjoy consuming more humor. All you need to do is find a TV show, performance, or video clip where there are jokes being told in a traditional format with a setup followed by a punchline. If you're not familiar with this structure, here's an example from Jerry Seinfeld:

Setup

> "According to most studies, people's No. 1 fear is public speaking. Number two is death."

Punchline

> "This means, to the average person, if you go to a funeral, you're better off in the casket than doing the eulogy."

Some of the best places to find jokes being delivered in this structured way are late night talk show monologues (like Stephen Colbert or Jimmy Kimmel), satire news programs (like *The Daily Show* or

Saturday Night Live's Weekend Update), or award shows and banquets (like the *Academy Awards* or the *White House Correspondence Dinner*). Most of these shows use the format where they will simply read a headline from the news or introduce a popular topic, and then make a joke about it. All you need to do is pause the video after the setup and see if you can guess some possible punchlines. It's a lot of fun to do it with other people in the room with you. Here's an example from the *Tonight Show* with Jimmy Fallon:

> "A French company is developing a robot that will tuck kids into bed and read them bedtime stories."

NOW IS WHEN YOU WOULD HIT PAUSE. . . .

Now think of some possible punchlines. Think about the absurdity in that. What is weird, infuriating, whimsical, or hilarious about it to you? What could go wrong? Try thinking about what types of things kids say and do or things robots say and do. What would it be like for the parents? Then, give your best shot at a funny punchline. Got anything?

These are more difficult to do if you've already heard or read the punchline, so it's best to learn to pause it at the right time so you have a clean slate to work with. For example, I already knew the punchline so I had a tough time with this one. Initially I thought of the concept of it being a "dead-bot dad" (instead of dead-beat dad), but I didn't think that was too funny. Or since it was a French study, I thought it could be called a "Lazy Faire (Laissez-Faire)" approach to parenting—again, meh. Finally, I thought the robot will read children's books like "One fish, Two fish, three hundred to the tenth power divided by the hypotenuse fish" and "The Little Engine that Could Rise up and Destroy Humanity." Okay, getting a little better. What did you come up with?

Here's the full joke from Fallon:

Setup: "A French company is developing a robot that will tuck kids into bed and read them bedtime stories."

Punchline: "Kids are calling it a cool and innovative thing to eventually discuss with their therapists."

If yours isn't perfect at first, don't sweat it. Again, it's the exercise that's important. You're simply training your brain to think more humorously and look at life through a funnier filter. Remember:

Humor is not a talent. **Humor is a habit.**

The cool thing about guessing the punchline humor habit is that a setup can have multiple punchlines, so if you're doing it alone you can keep trying until you find one you like, or if you're doing it with friends, everyone can take a shot at it. On one Weekend Update segment of *Saturday Night Live*, the anchor Seth Meyers performed the setup, delivered the punchline, and was then joined by former Weekend Update anchors Tina Fey, Amy Poehler, and Jimmy Fallon for a "Joke Off" where they just kept trying to come up with more punchlines to the setup—essentially this exercise! You can Google *Saturday Night Live* Weekend Update Joke Off and check it out. Watching it will make you feel better about trying this humor habit as some of their punchlines are hilarious and others are . . . well, like finding your six-pack abs. (If you do watch it, just FYI, it's probably not one to watch at work or with the kids.)

Caption This

This exercise was referred to earlier from the study where researchers studied brain scans. The great thing is you can do this exercise on your own without loaning your brain to science. All you need to do is come up with funny captions to cartoons. The easiest way to get good blank cartoons is by doing *The New Yorker* magazine caption contest. Each week they have a blank cartoon and allow anyone to create funny captions. You can submit yours with a chance to have it published or you can simply play along on your own without submitting. You can find the contest at newyorker.com/cartoons/contest or play on Instagram @neworkercartoons.

If you want to do this habit more than once per week, you can always look at past caption contests on *The New Yorker* and place a sticky note on your screen over the caption while you try to come up with your own. You can also Google "blank cartoons to caption" or "stock cartoons." You'll get a mix of some with and without captions, but plenty to play with. Another way to practice this habit is with photos on social media. Rather than posting that perfect photo of you and your friends having cocktails at the beach with the caption "Sunday Funday!" or "#Blessed!"—find a photo that's a little awkward or funny, and try to think of a funny caption to go along with it. Maybe there's one photo where you weren't ready, your eyes are half closed, and you look like you just ate a lemon. Post that one with a caption like "Had a great time at the beach—just forgot to tell my face." Feel free to get your friends in the mix by posting a funny photo and asking them to caption it for you.

Hashtag Games

This is kind of a niche habit that works really well if you use social media. There are all sorts of accounts where you try to be creative and come up with the funniest or wittiest hashtag based on the topic. Jimmy Fallon is the most popular account on Twitter (or X, or whatever it's called when you read this book) that does this but there are a lot of others. For example, one of the hashtags was #MakeAMovieChristmas. Then people would tweet movie titles that they tweak in order to make it Christmas-themed. "A Nightmare on Elf Street," "Harry Potter and the Chamber of Secret Santas," and "Thor: Ragnarockin' around the Christmas Tree." Another example is #RejectedSuperheroes and people came up with "The Dad Joker," "The Hot Flash," and "Super Mansplainer." If you don't have a Twitter (or X) account but want to play, you can search "Jimmy Fallon Hashtags" and all the old segments are on YouTube. Just like in "Guess the Punchline," you can pause the video after you hear the hashtag to come up with a few of your own before hearing what others came up with.

Sharpening your funny focus through these humor habits is all about creating new thinking patterns in the brain. The neurons in your brain will begin to fire on the funny in your life more and more often, and according to Hebbian's theory, "neurons that fire together, wire together."[10] With consistency, you'll literally change the way your brain processes information and eventually become hardwired for humor. Creating a funny focus is about being intentional and not simply hoping for humor, but harnessing it.

Humor Homework

Develop a Funny Focus

Choose as many of the following Humor Habits as you'd like to complete and write about how they went. If you complete more than three, then put on a hoodie with the hood up, do a few boxing moves, and yell "I am the greatest!" If people look at you weird, it's okay. They're jealous.

3 Funny Things Intervention (A One-Week Challenge)

Each day for one week, write down three things you found funny, absurd, humorous, or amusing—it will make you happier! Perhaps it made you laugh out loud, smirk, or just think to yourself, "That's pretty funny." In the rare chance you aren't carrying this book with you everywhere you go like a retriever with a new Frisbee, you might use the notes app or voice memo feature on your phone to document the funny stuff so you don't forget!

Day 1

1 ______________ 2 ______________ 3 ______________

______________ ______________ ______________

______________ ______________ ______________

Day 2

1 ______________ 2 ______________ 3 ______________

______________ ______________ ______________

______________ ______________ ______________

Day 3

1 ______________ 2 ______________ 3 ______________

______________ ______________ ______________

______________ ______________ ______________

Day 4

1 ______________ 2 ______________ 3 ______________

______________ ______________ ______________

______________ ______________ ______________

Day 5

1 ______________ 2 ______________ 3 ______________

______________ ______________ ______________

______________ ______________ ______________

Day 6

1 ______________ 2 ______________ 3 ______________

______________ ______________ ______________

______________ ______________ ______________

Day 7

1 ______________ 2 ______________ 3 ______________

______________ ______________ ______________

______________ ______________ ______________

Reflect: What was it like to try to find three funny things each day? Did it get easier as the week went along? How did you feel by the end of the week? How do you feel looking back at your list?

____

____

____

____

____

____

Humor Jar

STEP 1: Find a container (jar, basket, etc.).

STEP 2: Decide where you'll place the jar and who will be participating. (Is this just for you in your office? For the whole family in the kitchen? For colleagues and team members in the work meeting room?)

STEP 3: Explain the activity to participants.

STEP 4: Place the slips of paper and pen next to the jar and start playing!

STEP 5: Based on how many people are participating and how many slips you're collecting, determine when and how often you'll take the slips out and read them. Have fun and get creative with this! If it's at work, do it during a potluck or party. If it's at home, make it part of a date night or family night!

*Great question, from the front row—yes, if you're doing the Three Funny Things one-week challenge, you can add those to your humor jar for that week—particularly if they involve others who are participating. Your humor jar will continue all year-long, so you will have plenty more entries to add.

Reflect during the Humor Jar: What have you noticed about yourself while doing this activity? What have you noticed about others who are participating?

____

____

____

____

____

____

Reflect after reading the slips: What was it like to go back and read through all your funniest moments from the year/quarter/month? Did you forget some of them? Do you notice any themes about what you find the funniest? What was it like to share this experience with others if you did?

____

____

____

____

____

____

Mirthful Mantra

STEP 1: Come up with a mirthful mantra you would like to try. Remember the categories to help you find one: Movie Mantras, Sarcastic Singing, Inside Jokes, and Serious Mantra Makeovers. Don't get paralyzed by permanence, you can always try a new one!

My Mirthful Mantra to try is: ____________________

____

STEP 2: Put it somewhere that you will see it often, like a sticky note on your desk, in your wallet or purse, bathroom mirror, and so on.

STEP 3: Say it a few times per day randomly or when you see your note—just to get used to saying it.

STEP 4: Start saying it when things get stressful or you're getting irritated. C'mon, say it with feeling! Remember, you can always let others in on it—it may become a group mantra!

Reflect: If you used your Mirthful Mantra during a stressful time, what was it like? How did it affect you in the moment? What about later?

___

___

___

___

___

___

___

From Seeing Funny to Being Funny

NOTE: In Chapter 12, you'll learn some "Humor Hacks" and techniques from the world of comedy writing to help you create humor from personal struggles. Go ahead and try the rest of your Humor Homework for this chapter now, and you can also come back and try them again after learning more Humor Hacks in Chapter 12!

Humorous Reappraisal (What I Could've Said Game)

Think of one mildly stressful event from the past few weeks that has upset you or you've had trouble letting go.

What was the situation?

___

What did you say or do?

____

____

What could you have done or said to add a little humor to the situation? Feel free to add a few. It's okay if you don't think of anything at first. Call a funny friend and ask them to help you come up with a humorous reappraisal for your situation.

____

____

____

____

____

____

Reflect: What was it like to try to view the situation from a different lens? Was it difficult to find a funny focus? How does this exercise impact how you feel when thinking back on the situation now?

____

____

____

____

____

____

Guess the Punchline

Find a late-night talk show, satire news show, or comedy special you like that includes jokes with standard setups and punchlines. Then just hit pause after the setup and see if you and/or your friends and family can come up with witty punchlines. The best part is, whether you come up with something or not, you get to hit play and hear the punchline anyway! Here are a couple of jokes in writing to get you started.

From Tina Fey and Amy Poehler as they hosted the 2014 Golden Globe Awards:

Setup: "Matthew McConaughey is being praised for his role in *Dallas Buyers Club* where he lost 45 pounds."

PAUSE AND THINK OF POSSIBLE PUNCHLINES

Got anything? Write it here:

____

Beginning of Punchline: "Or as actresses call it. . ."

PAUSE AND THINK OF POSSIBLE WAYS TO FINISH THIS PUNCHLINE

Got anything? Write it here:

____

End of Punchline: ". . .being in a movie."

Notice that this particular joke gives two opportunities for you to pause and think of a punchline. Many of the jokes in this format provide that option, so take advantage! You can pause it right after the setup to take your punchline in any direction you want, or if they begin the punchline with "or as ____ calls it" or "parents are saying ________", etc., you can pause it there to finish off the punchline they started.

Okay, one more for fun before you're off to find a show to do the homework with. This is from *The Tonight Show* with Jimmy Fallon:

Setup: Starbucks is now banning smoking within 25 feet of its stores.

PAUSE AND THINK OF POSSIBLE PUNCHLINES

Got anything? Write it here: ______________________
____

Punchline: Which will get worse for smokers when they realize every Starbucks is about 25 feet from another Starbucks.

Reflect: After doing this activity, what was it like to hear common or unfunny topics and headlines read and then trying to look at them with a funny focus?

____
____
____
____
____
____

Caption This

Go to newyorker.com/humor or @newyorkercartoons on instagram and browse through some of the cartoons and try to come up with a caption to this week's cartoon! Or simply Google blank cartoons to practice with. (Hint: sometimes with captions and humor in general, it helps to focus on real feelings, situations, and relationships people deal with)

Remember, if you had trouble coming up with something clever—at this point it's more about challenging your brain to think in this way. It might take some consistent workouts before you're comfortable enough to rip your shirt off and flaunt that humor muscle six-pack.

Reflect: As you browse through cartoons, are there certain types of humor or common themes you're noticing you're drawn to? What is it like to do some of these exercises alone versus with others?

____
____
____
____
____
____
____

Hashtag games

Come up with as many fun answers as you can to the following hashtags. If you need to Google some book or movie titles to get the wheels turning, go for it! It's just about getting your brain to have fun playing with words, rhymes, and meanings.

#MakeAChildrensBookScary
Example: Furious George
Your answers: ____________________
____________________ ____________________
____________________ ____________________
____

#AddAWordImproveAMovie
Example: Cocaine Koala Bear
Your answers: ____________________
____________________ ____________________
____________________ ____________________
____

#ChangeALetterRuinAMovie
Example: Toy Gun (Top Gun)
Your answers: ______________________

______________________ ______________________
______________________ ______________________
____

Want to do more? Just search for hashtag games online!

Reflect: Out of all the Humor Homework exercises in this chapter, which are the toughest for you? Which are easiest? What does that tell you about your sense of humor? What have you learned about yourself from this chapter?

____
____
____
____
____
____
____

Bringing Humor to Work with L.A.F.T.E.R.

We spend more than one-third of our waking lives (about 115,000 hours) at work. In fact, the only place we spend more time than work is in bed.[1] If only we could find a way to combine the two—the ultimate productivity life hack! Perhaps one day, a neurosurgeon will be saying, "AI Bot, wake me up if there are any complications with this procedure," as they snore through a craniectomy. Until then, however, we need to be awake for those 115,000 hours—give or take a few under the desk snoozes (see *Seinfeld* episode "The Nap"). If you're a clock watcher, and the final three hours of your workday seem to drag along like udders on an earthworm, just wait until you calculate how many hours you have left until retirement. It's a serious amount of time to be serious all the time.

There are plenty of business reasons to curtail chronic seriousness and embrace a little levity at work. As we covered in Chapter 2, humor reduces stress and burnout, fosters connection, and boosts team engagement. Humor can also help you get hired and promoted! One major talent solutions and staffing survey found that 91% of executives believe that a sense of humor is important for career advancement, and 84% feel that people with a good sense of humor do a better job.[2] They're probably right, too, because a separate study on happiness and productivity used comedy to make people laugh resulting in a 12% increase in productivity.[3] Instead of motivational speakers and inspiration gurus, companies should just start having Amber Ruffin or Conan O'Brien host their team retreats.

But more important than the business case for humor at work is the human case. We're given a finite amount of time on Earth to savor the human experience, and a sense of humor (fun, levity, laughter, playfulness) is a vital part of that experience. To deprive ourselves of humor for a third of our lives is to crush the human spirit.

Any decent business or personal development book must have a clever model based on an acronym to help you remember the tools and strategies. In an effort to explain how to use humor at work, I figured a perfect acronym word to go along with humor is LAUGH-TER! Then I realized, that's too many letters for a simple word. Who decided we'd spell laughter that way? And why is there a huge *UGH* in the middle of it?

la-UGH-ter

How sad and draining. It's like if when something thrilling happened, we said it was. . .ex-SIGH-ting. I knew laughter wouldn't work for an acronym, so I decided as far as the *UGH* goes. . ."F" that.

There's our acronym: L.A.F.T.E.R.!

Lead by example

Ask for help

Fun over funny

Tell your story

Earn it

Rituals

6 Lead by Example

Using humor in more serious professional settings isn't some new phenomenon. In the famous Lincoln-Douglas debates in 1858, when Stephen A. Douglas accused Abraham Lincoln of being two-faced, Lincoln replied, "If I had two faces, do you think I would choose to wear this one?"[1] How great is that? He didn't take himself too seriously and played off his gawky appearance. Little did he know that face would go from being funny to being money! Lincoln understood the power of humor and its ability to provide a psychological reset. In cabinet meetings, he would often read humorous stories to ease his mind before addressing difficult issues or making important decisions. Before one cabinet meeting, he read from his favorite humorist and didn't understand why the cabinet failed to appreciate the humor as he did, stating:

> *"Gentlemen, why don't you laugh? With the fearful strain that is upon me night and day, if I did not laugh occasionally, I should die, and you need this medicine as much as I do."*[2]

If the president of a country that was being ripped apart by a civil war over the abolishment of slavery can find ways to harness the power of humor in his work, then surely you can too.

Also, did you notice how in this example President Lincoln was practicing the "collect and consume" type of humor habit from Chapter 4 and in the first example it was clear that he had a pretty well-developed "funny focus" from Chapter 5 by showing off his quick wit? If it isn't already obvious, the answer is yes. . . . I traveled back in time and gave him an advance copy of this book to prepare him for his presidency. Damn, I should have had him write an endorsement for the cover!

When it comes to humor, you don't need to be the leader of the free world to lead by example. In your organization, you may have a formal leadership role managing a team or perhaps you're in a brand-new entry-level position and don't supervise anyone. Based on the research shared in this chapter, if you aren't in a leadership position yet, you're more likely to be promoted to one after using the tools in this book (OMG, please let me know if that happens)! Whether you're the CEO or the new customer service representative, when it comes to bringing humor to work it's still important to lead by example. They say, "Your vibe attracts your tribe" (and by *they*, I think it's mostly Etsy wall art makers and Pinterest meme creators), but it's true. If you want to work in a place that's fun, where humor is valued, and people don't take themselves too seriously, then the best way to start is by leading the way. When you're "in good humor" and can leverage levity as a tool, team members, colleagues, and customers will follow your lead.

You've already started leading by example by reading this book. Specifically, the concepts about combating chronic seriousness are directly related to this section. The next step is developing levity as part of your work or leadership style much like people develop communication, delegating, or listening skills. The key to leading with levity is to find the sweet spot of confidence and humility (Figure 6.1). It takes both humility and confidence to showcase your fun, funny, and less serious side at work. Confidence without humility is arrogance, and humility without confidence is self-deprecation.

Confidence vs. Humility

	Low Humility	High Humility
High Confidence	**Arrogant** Chronic seriousness, impatience, lack of connection and empathy	**Leading with Levity** Respected, reliable, hard-working, fun, approachable, light-hearted
Low Confidence	**Insecure** Overly critical of self and others; highly concerned with what others think	**Self-deprecating** Lacks confidence and motivation; may seem too silly and untrustworthy

FIGURE 6.1 Using humor in leadership.

Confidence

Legendary New York Giants head coach Bill Parcells once said, "Confidence is born of demonstrated ability."[3] Generally, the more you've demonstrated your ability and reliability to perform your job well, the more confidence you'll have in yourself to showcase your humility through humor. That's not to say that humor *can't* be effective your first week on the job or even in an interview. After graduate school, I was interviewing to be a full-time residence director at the University of California, Riverside. A staff member drove me across campus in a sweet electric golf cart, and after I commented on it, they informed me that because I'd be on call for multiple buildings across campus, if I got the job, I'd actually get my own sweet ride! In the interview with the selection committee, their first question was: "Why are you interested in this position?" Before eventually answering the question seriously, I replied "Well, I've done a national search and narrowed it down to only institutions where I'd have my own golf cart." My comment got a laugh, and I got the job, and more importantly . . . the golf cart. Humor worked for me in that situation, but for many, a job interview is intimidating enough without also trying out bits. For most people, situations like job interviews, being in a new role, not feeling psychologically safe, or not feeling confident makes it very hard to use humor at first. That's okay. Just like any trait, humor comes more naturally to some than others. It's normal to feel more confident expressing your humorous side at work the more comfortable and competent you feel in your role.

Humility

At this point in human history, giving advice on how to be humble is among one of the least humble things I could do. It's like, "I know we've heard about humility from people like the Dalai Lama, Mother Theresa, and Gandhi, but I think it's time you've heard my perspective!" But the truth is, I'm not humble. At least, I don't think it's something that always comes naturally to me. I typically lean toward the "confidence" side of the continuum, and humility is something I have to intentionally cultivate and demonstrate. I've often wondered if I'm the only one or if others are like that as well. Some people say, "Oh, I don't need any recognition or awards." Well, I do. I'm a high achiever and I like being recognized for a job well done or winning things like an "Employee of the Year" award. Unfortunately, now that I work for myself, those types of accolades don't exist, so I did the only logical thing I could think of . . . and gave myself an award (Figure 6.2).

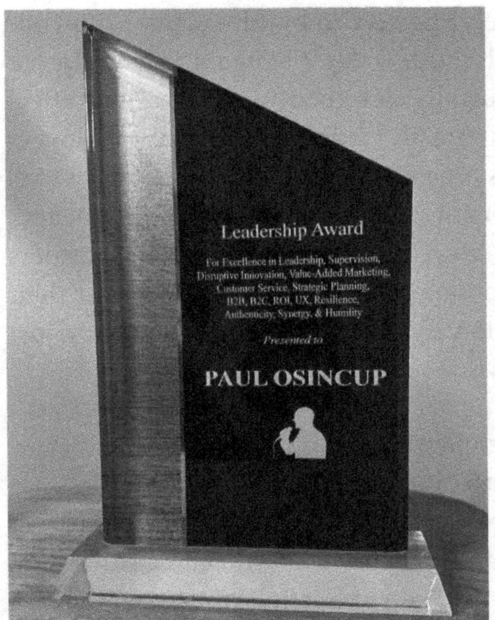

FIGURE 6.2 My own leadership award for "Excellence in Leadership, Supervision, Disruptive Innovation, Value-added Marketing, Customer Service, Strategic Planning, B2B, B2C, ROI, UX, Resilience, Authenticity, Synergy, & (of course) Humility."

It's so nice to have it sitting on my desk every day! Seriously, though, you don't need to win an award . . . you can literally buy one anywhere! I did, and it feels great. Although, if you do buy yourself an award, don't make the same mistake I did. I confirmed with the woman on the phone all the great things for the award to say and that it should read "Presented to: Paul Osincup." She said, "Great, you can pick it up in three days, and what's your name?" Cue Facepalm.

There are many books far more in-depth about the more "serious" ways to harness humility as a leader. But as a slightly overconfident trophy seeker, I've also found humor to be an effective means to modesty. As you'll see later in Chapter 10, one of the easiest and safest ways to use humor at work is to start with yourself. Humor or joking at your own expense is typically called "self-deprecating humor," which can be extremely effective in building trust with your team. In fact, research from the *Leadership & Organizational Development Journal* that was specifically designed to measure the effectiveness of self-deprecating humor in leaders found that employees rated managers who used this type of humor higher in their overall leadership ability and trustworthiness.[4] The best part is the research showed it didn't even matter how funny they were! When leaders don't take themselves too seriously, a little grace is given on their comedic chops. Your team knows you're not Chris Rock; they just want to make sure *you* know you're not The Rock.

Outside of the nerdy little humor world you've crawled into with me inside this book, when people refer to humor directed at yourself or joking about yourself, it's called self-deprecating humor—but I hate that term as an all-encompassing way to describe humor at one's own expense. Deprecation is when we belittle and express disapproval and sometimes disgust. That's a negative vibe to put out as a leader, and as you can see from Figure 6.1, it can come off as though you're searching for a compliment, lack seriousness, or are insecure. But not all humor about oneself needs to be to the level of deprecating. Researcher Rod Martin distinguished between more positive and negative types of self-deprecating humor, labeling them "self-defeating humor" and "self-enhancing humor."[5] I find this a much better way to think of it when attempting to make humor at your own expense in a professional environment. It is possible to find humor in the adversities of being you without belittling or demeaning yourself. Think of it like the difference between self-awareness and self-loathing. If we're chatting after I've had a large coffee and an onion bagel, and I'm self-aware, I may calmly slide a mint in my mouth. If I'm self-loathing, I'll pour dish detergent on my tongue and scrub it with a steel wool pad. The first one might make you feel appreciative or even more connected to me, the latter will make you wonder if I'm okay. Too many self-defeating jokes will typically make people feel uncomfortable, and you're more likely to get weird look than a laugh.

Here are a few examples of how to be more self-enhancing rather than self-defeating or deprecating:

- **Don't kill your skills.** Avoid jokes that directly connect with your ability or skills to do your job. For example, it's okay to make fun of yourself for dropping that jelly donut on your shirt if you're an investment banker, but perhaps not if you're a doctor. Nobody wants to hear their doctor say, "Sorry about the stain on my tie from that donut. I guess I'm just all butterfingers today!" right before their vasectomy.
- **Experiences over appearances.** The occasional joke about your appearance is fine (see next bullet), but if you can, lean more toward personal experiences like minor accidents, forgetful moments, or family funnies. For example, in a speech at the UK premier of *The Lord of the Rings: The Rings of Power,* Amazon CEO Jeff Bezos revealed that just before he met with the creative team to give them notes on the series, his son gave him one piece of advice that was to just not "eff up" the show.[6] The visual of one of the richest men in the world having a son who's embarrassed by him makes him seem more human and approachable, but we don't lose faith in his ability to run Amazon.
- **It's about confidence, not compliments.** Whether it's your looks (I often joke about being short and bald) or tough times you've been through, the topics of your self-directed humor should be about things you now feel confident or at least comfortable with yourself enough to joke about. When you make jokes about areas that you're still quite vulnerable or sensitive about, it will likely come through and may trigger people to feel sympathy for you, console you, or just feel awkward. The intent of the humor should be to share a laugh to connect with, engage, excite, or even disarm people, not to receive a compliment in return.
- **The higher our status, the more people laugh at us.** This section of the book is all about leading by example and that's where self-enhancing humor works best—when you're in a leadership role. The more power and influence you have, the more impact it

> will have when others see you taking yourself lightly. Remember, power and influence may come from formal titles, but it might also come from informal factors like how long you've worked in the company and inter-office dynamics. If you're in a lower status position, however, it may be important to use this type of humor carefully as it can backfire with lower-ranking individuals.[7]

While poking fun at yourself in a self-enhancing way is an easy and effective method to start leading by example with humor, there are plenty of other ways that don't involve you being a punchline.

Participation > Permission

In my work with the international work culture consulting firm Delivering Happiness, one thing we've learned over years of work with hundreds of companies from a multitude of industries is that most culture initiatives fail because of a lack of leadership buy-in. It's fruitless to have an employee culture committee create organizational value statements if the CEO doesn't champion the cause, give some input, or show at least a little investment. Simply "allowing" the team to take on initiatives like this but not participating in some way is the leadership version of Alexis from the TV series *Schitt's Creek* saying, "Oh my god, I love that for you," in her quasi-charming yet condescending way. In just about any book on leadership, you'll find some form of the philosophy that a leader should not expect their team to do anything they are not willing to do themselves. It goes a long way when the division vice president comes in on Saturday to help the team push a project through or is seen setting up chairs with the events crew for a symposium. The same concept holds true for humor in a work environment. I've worked with countless leaders who encourage their team to use humor and have fun at work, but don't understand why it doesn't happen.

The regional manager of a bank I worked with told me she had a couple of branch managers who were excited about incorporating more humor at work. They approached her about making a calendar with funny photos and memes of team members based on the themes of the month that would be on display in the lobby of their branches. She thought it was a great idea and told them to go for it, but it never came to fruition. She said this wasn't the first time this type of thing happened and that although she has high expectations of her team and suffers from a bit of chronic seriousness herself, she wanted her team to feel free to have fun and use humor to enhance the work environment. The problem was that her team had a *sense* of humor, but not a *sensei* of humor. Essentially, she was saying, "OMG, a funny office calendar? I love that for you!" The manager didn't have to participate by being "Miss April Fools" in a goofy photo for the calendar if she wasn't comfortable with that. Participation can also mean empowering them with a small budget, some dedicated time to talk about it during a meeting or connecting them with the company digital media team. She could have helped brainstorm themes or costumes for them, or simply showed enthusiasm to show up and laugh with them at the photo shoots. There are plenty of ways to be involved in the humor happenings without completely jumping out of your comfort zone (more on this in Chapter 8).

When you pair your permission with your participation, you'll see an increase in engagement because the team members feel safer playing *along* with you rather than playing *in front* of you. You can remember this by using the Four Ps Formula shown in Figure 6.3.

It's because of the need for trust and psychological safety (fine, I'll spell it correctly) that when I'm speaking at an event or facilitating a workshop, I always try to engage the leader(s) as early on as possible.

Several years back, I was the keynote speaker for the Disaster Recovery Journal (DRJ) World Conference. The audience was about 1,000 business continuity and disaster recovery professionals (think risk assessment and emergency planning) from a variety of industries. They all had serious jobs and jet-lagged brains, and I could almost feel the gravity of their thoughts as they walked in and were taking a final moment to check emails and sip coffee. The energy was heavy and quiet, but at least my talk about humor and happiness was in a dimly lit hotel ballroom, at 8:00 a.m, . . . oh, and interactive! Ugh,

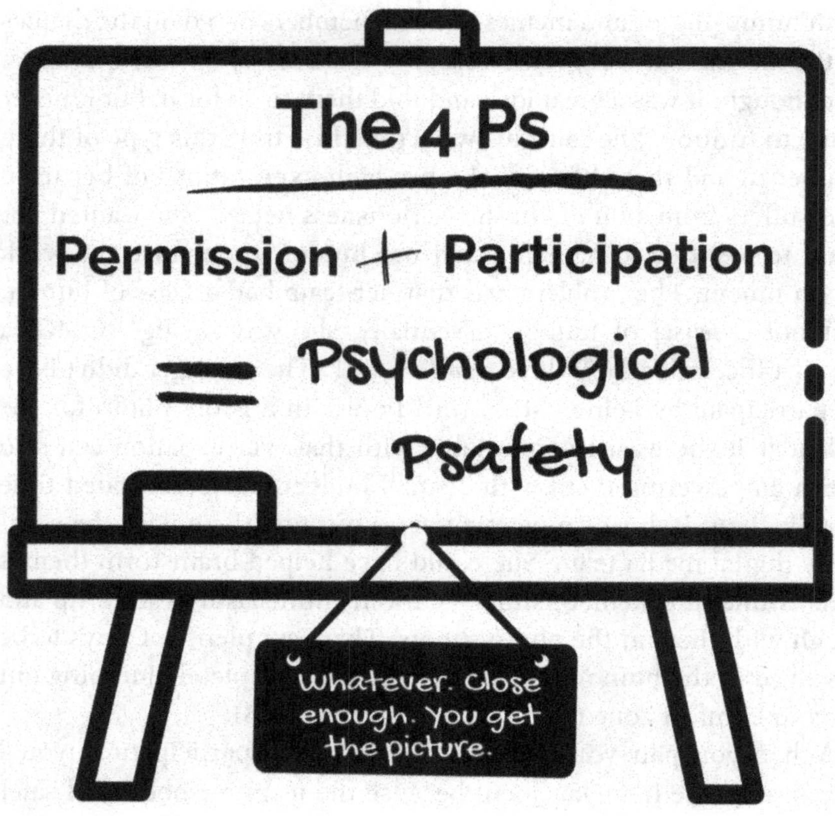

FIGURE 6.3 Four Ps Formula.

what a disaster. Except it wasn't. Over the course of the hour, the participants warmed up, connected, laughed, and learned from each other. I mean, if I told you it ended with a standing ovation, you'd think I was being cocky or I was lying, so I'm not going to say that. But I'm not lying, and I already told you I wasn't humble!

I believe the success of that talk, however, began and hinged not on me, but on the CEO of DRJ, Bob Arnold. Bob is a hardworking, well-respected leader who doesn't need to be the center of attention. That being said, he agreed ahead of time to come on stage at the beginning of my talk to have a little fun. I told him and the crowd that since talking about humor at a business disaster recovery conference at 8 a.m. involved a high amount of risk, before I would begin my keynote, I would need him to sign a "Keynote Disaster Recovery Plan." The plan stated that since the whole "Humor & Happiness" at 8 a.m. thing was his idea, he would be held liable for any keynote disaster that may occur. It included language like:

> *"If an opening keynote disaster is imminent, the DRJ Fall World Conference business immediately functions at the alternate site location . . . the hotel bar."*
>
> And . . .
>
> *"You personally assume responsibility for anything that may materially and adversely affect my ability to deliver this talk as previously planned. Such events may include one or more of the following: natural or human-made disasters (including fire, flood, earthquake, failed jokes, or a nonresponsive audience)."*

Bob laughed as he signed his life away in front of the crowd and the crowd laughed along with him. I had not done much of anything yet, but the crowd had already changed. By playing along and participating in my foolishness, Bob signaled to the participants that it's not only encouraged, but safe to do so.

Whether it's a large conference or a smaller department or team, the same participation principle applies. In fact, when I facilitate workshops with smaller groups, I've noticed the power of participation from leadership has a greater impact. Many well-meaning leaders will stop into a departmental workshop or team retreat briefly to show their support. Typically, they'll stand in the back of the room, not wanting to interrupt or distract from what is going on. Early on in my career, I would simply continue with what we're already doing, but over the years I've found that when people are engaged in an activity, whether humor-related or something more serious, a leader entering the room and not participating has a chilling effect on participants. Now, as a facilitator I ask for leadership participation ahead of time and give ideas for specific portions of the workshop that could be beneficial for them to participate in. Or, if the leader pops in unexpectedly, I will welcome them, explain what we're doing, and ask them to jump in. As a leader, even if you can't join the team for the entire event (whether it's a communication workshop, retreat, or Taco and Trivia Tuesday), you can plan to participate at a key time by connecting with the event planner or facilitator.

Finding the right balance between confidence and humility, adding a touch of self-enhancing humor, and pairing permission with participation will help you add a little more levity to your leadership style. You don't have to be the next Abraham Lincoln to lead by example with humor, but if you are, I hope you get immortalized on something cool like cryptocurrency, the Venmo logo, or Kohl's cash.

Humor Homework

Bringing Humor to Work

Lead by Example

Make a list of traits or characteristics about yourself that you could joke about at work.

(What's difficult about being you or your situation? Are you clumsy? Are you very short, tall, big, small, bald, hairy? Do you look like a certain celebrity? Do you talk too much or not at all? Think about things that have happened to you or dumb things you've done. Does your car always break down? Were you the one who microwaved fish in the break room?)

____

____

____

Now, circle the ones that you feel self-confident enough in to joke with colleagues about. Cross out any that might make you feel uneasy or self-conscious (when in doubt, cross it out). Cross out any that specifically undermine the skills necessary to do your job (like joking about having poor listening skills if you're a therapist or the fact that you can't see if you drive a bus). Now you have a list for some possible topics to joke at your own expense about at work. Keep this list to use in Chapter 12, where you'll learn how to create humor out of these topics!

Post a funny photo of yourself on social media or send it to a few trusted colleagues in an email and ask people to write a funny caption for it. Ask people who your celebrity doppelganger is. Did you do it? If so, how did it feel? What was the best response?

7 Ask for Help

Chef Russell Scott is one of only 67 Certified Master Chefs in the United States. He has been the executive chef at some of the most prestigious restaurants, hotels, and country clubs in the country, and he won two gold medals as a member of the U.S. team at the International Culinary Olympics in Germany. (Yes, there's a Culinary Olympics. It's like the regular Olympics but more dangerous. Instead of a baton, the relay team passes a knife.) Chef Scott was my boss at the Culinary Institute of America in Napa, California, where he served as the Dean of Education and I was Associate Dean for Student Affairs. Culinary culture is structured and formal by design, and just like your favorite cooking TV shows, everything is "Yes, Chef!" "Right away Chef!" and is reminiscent of a military chain of command. Chef Scott did remind me of a general at times in his uniform with a perfectly pressed dress shirt, shiny black shoes, and newly steamed chef whites. He tried to model the dress code, his high regard for the profession, and his high standards to the students and chef instructors at the institution.

I'll never forget my second day of work when he asked me to stop by his office. I thought, "Oh, he wants to check in and see how things are going for me . . . how sweet!" Not quite. I mean, he did ask how things were going, but what got my attention was when he asked,

"What's going on with this?" as he pointed at the five o'clock shadow of stubble on my face. He proceeded to tell me that he couldn't enforce the dress code with the students (which included that they be clean shaven) if I came to work with stubble. I was bummed because I was going for a rugged Jason Statham or George Clooney vibe—plus I was lazy. He also informed me that one of the chefs kept a razor in his desk (but no shaving cream) in case I forgot again in the future. I never forgot. Clearly, he was serious about his job and could be an intimidating figure. Which is why it still surprises me that as our relationship grew, instead of getting upset, he would simply shake his head and smile when I would pop into his office and shout "What's up, Dean of Cuisine!?"

Despite his deliberate and well-ordered ways, I could see that he had a great sense of humor, and it became more common for us to have a laugh in his office from time to time. One day, Chef Scott said to me, "Paul, you joke around with me and bust my chops at times, but none of the other staff members do that. Why do you think that is?" I told him it was because he's scary and carries knives. It was clear that although Chef Scott needed to maintain the proper culinary hierarchy, he also wanted some of the other staff to see at least a small glimpse of his not-so-serious side occasionally. Then, he did something that stuck with me for years—he asked for my help. As I was leaving his office he said, "Well, feel free to do that in front of the team from time to time. You know, have fun at my expense." Even in the moment I thought this was brilliant. He wanted to show the team that he could take a joke and didn't always take things so seriously, but was self-aware enough to know that cracking jokes in the middle of a meeting or planning out humorous things to do wasn't necessarily his forte.

One day during our monthly staff meeting, Chef Scott was speaking on the importance of staff and students taking pride in their surroundings. He went on to give examples about the little things like pushing in the chairs that are strewn about in the common area as we pass through or picking up a piece of trash on the outside of the building. He then said he sees drops of water all over the bathroom counters and mirrors. He said while he's in there, he will take a paper towel and wipe the counter and then scrub the mirror. I interjected, "Chef, you know it doesn't matter how hard you scrub the mirror, it will still be that same reflection staring back at you, right?" The entire room fell silent and my colleagues looked at me like, "I'll help you pack up your office." Chef Scott broke the silence with a smile, head nod, and soft chuckle. "Yeah, Hehe. Good one." That was followed by a collective sigh of relief and laughs from the rest of the team. Chef Scott already had the authority and reverence part of his leadership recipe dialed in, but by asking for help to add a little humor at his own expense, he was able to compliment it with another pinch of humility and dash of authenticity.

Renee, the executive director of a state government agency, used this same tactic in a different way to ease some tension that was building within her team. The annual retreat was typically a couple of hours away in the mountains at a nice resort, and the staff enjoyed it as a rare treat. That year, to reduce costs and because she thought it might be nice for the team to stay closer to home, the retreat took place in a bland meeting room at the community college a few miles from their office. The retreat had a Disney-inspired theme and as I arrived early to set up to facilitate their retreat, I immediately saw Renee in a busy and loud Disney Princess Hawaiian shirt for the occasion. She and her assistant director were talking about how discouraged the staff was about the retreat setting—and they hadn't even seen the sad looking meeting room yet! The assistant director joked, "Way to go, Renee! What, was the conference room at the county detention center not available?" The three of us laughed, but then Renee said to her AD, "You should use that! When you get things started, just call out the elephant in the room and give me crap for it."

The light roast of Renee got a laugh exactly as planned, with the AD adding, "I know Renee feels bad we didn't go somewhere cooler this year. When we got here, she told me, 'I think I made a big mistake.' I told her . . . 'You sure did, but it's okay, I have a shirt you can borrow.'" The jokes momentarily lowered the tension with the staff enough that it gave Renee a chance to remark from the side, "I know it's just not the same. I owe you guys! I'll make it up to you!" Do you remember the improv comedy principle from Chapter 3 about noticing gifts? Renee treated her retreat planning mistake as a gift. There was no time to look back and beat herself up about the mistake she made. Much like in an improv scene, she had to roll with the situation and find a way to turn it into a gift. It gave her an opportunity to show her team that she isn't perfect and can take a joke, as well as an excuse to do something nice for them later after telling them she owes them.

Punch It Up

Asking for help isn't just about having a colleague roast you to reduce the tension or make you more approachable. CEOs and even politicians often get a little humor help with the concept of "punching it up." They start with their first draft of a speech or presentation, and then ask a humorist or speechwriter to punch it up and add a little humor to it.

You can punch up just about any area of your job. The best way to do this is to begin with boring. Whether you're writing a speech, presentation, blog post, employee orientation manual, or a meeting agenda, begin with the boring version of it and get help punching it up afterward. Not only does this take the pressure off you to be hilarious, but it also enables you to be sure you've covered the necessary learning objectives or content first without getting distracted by the humor. This strategy doesn't have to be reserved just for writing projects either as you can punch up your office activities, retreats, trainings, and overall culture. Here are some resources to help you punch things up:

- **Internet Inspiration:** Don't be afraid to look to the internet for inspiration for that next presentation. Look up architecture and construction memes if you're speaking to a group of architects, find that perfect clip from *The Office* to begin your next employee training, or play a funny TikTok about the pain of a poorly run meeting at the beginning of your next meeting (ahem, I know a guy who made one): https://www.tiktok.com/@paulosincup/video/7187964022573010219

- **Ask AI:** Having a lot of problems you can't solve on your own just means you're human . . . or a math book. Okay, that math book joke you just read was adapted from something I got from ChatGPT. I prompted it to "write something funny about asking for help" and this is what it came up with: "Why did the math book ask for help? Because it had too many problems and couldn't solve them all on its own."[1] I didn't love the dad joke format of the ChatGPT version so I used a "Humor Hack" you'll learn about in Chapter 12 to reword it to something I liked a little better. (Feel free to come back after you read Chapter 12 and see if you can tell which humor hack I used)! Because I'm a proud comedian and writer, this is the first time I ever used open AI to source content, as the No. 1 sin in comedy is stealing material. But you're likely not a comedian. You're a sales manager or a nurse or a vice president of executive strategic content of an industry I haven't heard of yet. Whatever your role, there's nothing wrong with using AI to get a funny idea for your end-of-the-year banquet speech or your weekly team meeting.
- **The Company Comedian:** Incorporating more humor into your work doesn't have to be a covert mission. Let your team know this is important to you and ask for their help. In any organization, for every serious leader who doesn't have natural comedic chops or feels too busy to worry about humor, there's that . . . "one person." They're always making people laugh either with their gregarious larger-than-life persona or with their quick dry wit. Chances are this person is already sharing the latest funny memes and videos with colleagues and is often seen surrounded by colleagues holding court during lunch breaks. Why not tap into their excess energy and bandwidth by asking for their help in punching up your next presentation or task them with adding two minutes of humor to the beginning of each staff meeting?

The odds are pretty good that they'll jump at the opportunity, and it will help them focus their humorous abilities on creating traction instead of distraction.

- **Outside Experts:** Much like leaders who have people punch up their speeches, you can acquire professionals to help you add some laughs to the leadership retreat—and it doesn't have to be as a speechwriter. Whether you're looking to hire a keynote speaker, corporate trainer, team-building company, executive coach, or a consultant, if you truly believe humor will add value for you or your team, then it should be a criterion for hiring them. Let them know you want it to be lighthearted and fun, and ask them about how they add humor or fun into their offerings.

If humor isn't your natural strength, then treat it like you would any other skill. Work on improving it (i.e., this book), while also surrounding yourself with people who are strong in that area. You can delegate the humor responsibilities while continuing to learn from them, and use other resources to bring some funny to where you make your money.

Humor Homework

Ask for Help

Ask at least one person at work for help in one of the following ways:

- Tell them you're reading this book and want to develop your sense of humor and you'd like them to help you not take things so seriously. Have them gently tease you from time to time, or be your work "Humor Homie" and share funny content back and forth.

- Have a colleague help you "punch up" a document, email, presentation, or meeting agenda to make it more fun or funny. Okay, fine, half points if you have AI help.
- Have a colleague help you initiate some of the ideas from this book for bringing humor to work.

Reflect: Since you've talked to a colleague about intentionally using humor more, what have you noticed about your interactions? Are they more lighthearted in nature? Are you sharing funny stories, memes, or videos more? Are they following you around like a puppy now because you're the cool one at work? Probably.

____

____

____

____

____

____

8 Fun over Funny

At some point when reading this book or perhaps when you first saw it, you may have thought, "Humor is great and all, but I just don't think I'm that funny." If you're thinking that . . . you could be right. Maybe you're not very funny. I doubt it, but I haven't met you, so who knows? But if you're thinking that, you're at least humble and self-aware, which are both key ingredients to being funny. While there are tools in this book to help you learn to be funny, and developing your sense of humor will lead to you being funnier more often, one trick to discovering humor more frequently at work or home is to think *fun* over funny. Humor and fun aren't the same thing, but they often show up at the same parties. Think about the last time you and your colleagues or friends were doing something fun. Was there laughter? Usually when we get people together doing fun things, funny stuff happens, the funny people say funny things, or we simply start laughing for no real reason other than we're having fun. So, if fun leads to humor and laughter, then why not add more fun to that place where you spend a third of your life? (No, not your bedroom—totally different book.)

For some reason, in the past few years, the concept of fun at work has taken a public relations beating. Well, specifically the Ping-Pong table. During the tech boom, it became in vogue for tech companies (think Google) to adorn their corporate campuses with fun things like bean bag chairs, slides, board game rooms, and yes, Ping-Pong tables. What's weird to me is the number of articles that have come out in the past few years with titles like "RIP to the Ping-Pong Table" and "Culture Is More than Just a Ping-Pong Table," and "Did Ping-Pong Tables Start the Pandemic?" Okay, the last one is made up, but there are seriously hundreds of Ping-Pong-table–bashing articles out there! The two main premises I take away from most of these articles is that 1) a Ping-Pong table might not be everyone's version of fun at work, and 2) people need more than a Ping-Pong table or what it represents (fun) to feel valued at their job. (I mean, some of these articles even have the audacity to suggest that people value basic respect over Ping-Pong. What!? Yeah, right. They must have just interviewed people who suck at ping pong.) For the record, I agree with both of those two premises. First, it is important to find the right type of fun for yourself and/or your team at work. Second, no Ping-Pong table will make up for toxic colleagues, a boss with a bad temper, or people who use the breakroom microwave to cook fish. It isn't about the Ping-Pong table. It's about the environment it's put into and the way it's used. Putting *fun* into dys*fun*ction still makes it dysfunction.

There is, however, plenty of research about the benefits of a fun workplace. According to *Fortune*'s Great Place to Work 2023 study, out of all the drivers of workplace well-being, including things like pay, benefits, flexible schedules, trust, and fairness, the No. 1 driver of well-being at work for employees of all ages is . . . fun.[1] And it's not like this is a small study of 10 people from five different age brackets. This is from generational data collected from 1,195,669 employees from a diverse array of industries. That's a ton of fun. This also isn't a one-off weird year. These statistics are similar year to year. Eighty-one percent of employees who worked at companies that earned the distinction "Great Places to Work" said they worked in a fun environment, while only 62% of employees at companies in the next tier down (ranked as good) said the same. That 19-point disparity is the largest gap for any one marker of workplace well-being in the survey.[2] A good place to work must include things like excellent communication, fairness, inclusion, and trust, but from this research, once you have a good foundation in place, the largest factor that separates organizations from good to great is the fun factor. I'm no attorney, but if I were I would represent Ping-Pong tables in a class action defamation suit; I'd *serve* those papers so fast their heads would *spin*.

The *Fun*damentals of Fun

When I speak about humor and fun at work, people often want me to simply give them a list of fun things to do or try at their organization. While I don't mind doing so, it isn't necessarily the best method to initiating and encouraging fun because every person and organization is different. But fine—later in this chapter there's a list of 101 ways to have fun at work that you can dabble with and try. Before you dive into that, however, it's important to first consider these fundamentals of fun:

- ***Your* fun is *your* responsibility.** Even if you have a very serious job or you work in an organization that you wouldn't classify as good, let alone great—you can still choose to have fun during your workday. Take former U.S. Secretary of State Madeleine Albright, for example. She once decided to make her day a little more fun just for her own amusement. After the Gulf War, the Iraqi media and Saddam Hussein compared her to an "unparalleled serpent." Secretary Albright often wore decorative pins on her blouses, so at her next meeting with Iraq she showed up adorned with a snake pin. This was just the beginning of a fun ritual she created for herself in a very intense and stressful job. She went on to wear flowers and butterflies on good days, bugs when talking to nations she knows bugged the United States, and mushrooms on days when there were private negotiations happening because mushrooms do better in the dark.[3]

Rather than be sad that her job was too serious to have fun, Secretary Albright took her fun into her own hands.

Fun on a personal level is really about a mindset. It's the difference between being a thermometer or a thermostat. A thermometer tells the temperature (my boss sucks, I had to work an extra shift, or the stupid new software program doesn't work), but a thermostat can do something to positively impact the situation—even if just by one degree. There will be some forms of fun that won't fly at your workplace, there will be some that might work, and there will be some that nobody could stop you from doing (like reciting your mirthful mantra in your head during a boring meeting, reading your emails to yourself as Elmo or Jim Carrey, or almost any of the humor habits in this book). Focus on the fun you *can* do whether anyone else knows or not and then *choose* to make those things part of your day.

It turns out this intentional autonomy is important to our well-being, and specifically, to how we recover from work breaks. Research has found that people who made an autonomous choice of what to do on their lunch breaks recovered better from work-related stress.[4] For example, you already learned that watching humorous videos on your break can increase your productivity, but what is also important is that you're choosing to do so. The intentional choice will impact the quality of that break differently than, say, mindlessly scrolling through Instagram. If it is something that is fun to you and you are choosing to do it, then it will be a more restorative break. So rather than finding yourself in a dust storm of negativity with a few coworkers bitching about that brutal meeting, *choose* to grab lunch with your work bestie, read a book, knit, walk outside, practice your putting stroke, or watch the live stream video of the Cat Café. No matter your work scenario, take charge of your own workplace well-being and make ***your* fun *your* responsibility.**

- **Make it fun for *everyone*.** My friends and colleagues at The Fun Dept., a consulting firm focused solely on bringing fun into professional settings, have been delivering fun to workplaces for more than 20 years. What I love about their approach is that they've learned from their experience that fun must be all inclusive and nonthreatening. Nick Gianoulis, founder, CEO, and the "Godfather of Fun" at The Fun Dept. states, "Many team-building events are physical challenges that eliminate over 50% of your employee population from the get-go. Design activities that everyone can participate in and allow people to participate at their comfort level. Let people self-select their roles."[5] One of the reasons the Ping-Pong table got such a bad rap was because it became a symbol for forced or exclusive fun, and conjured images of a room filled with tech bros and "work hard, play harder" stenciled on the wall.

The goal of inclusive fun isn't to make it harder for you or your team to bring fun to work or to discourage certain types of activities, but rather, when planning an activity, to consider a few questions:

1. Will this be fun for most people? (If so, who may not find this fun?)
2. Are there accessibility issues (based on disabilities or time constraints for employees who work different shifts)?
3. How can we include those who may not be interested in this activity or may have accessibility issues?

Take, for example, two medical centers that were merging as one company but maintaining separate locations in the city. In an effort to build excitement for the change and encourage communication between the two facilities, they brought together both staff teams for a celebration and mixer at a local winery. It began with comments from the medical directors of each campus and they encouraged the teams to mingle with one another while enjoying the wine tastings and great food. Unfortunately, and somewhat predictably, people hung out in their comfort zones with their established cliques of work friends, the event felt more awkward than fun, and it didn't have the desired impact. The medical centers spent a lot of money on this event and definitely could have gotten more bang for their buck.

While an evening at a winery may sound fun to *most* of the team, there are those who have immediate obligations with kids after work or who may not drink alcohol. One possible way to make it more inclusive for those folks would have been to have a portion of the event on company time. Perhaps they could close the offices an hour early and have the event begin with some remarks and activities outside at the winery with a mix of beverages or no alcohol being served for the first 60–90 minutes. This would make it feel more welcoming to the alcohol-free employees and give employees who have after-work obligations time to be a part of the event. While after work may be the only option for certain activities or industries, typically making fun on company time increases engagement, makes it more inclusive, and feels like more of a treat to the employees. The leadership team could have also made it more inclusive for those who aren't as comfortable mingling in group settings with some simple activities. Perhaps a human bingo game with prizes where you find people who meet the criteria of each of your bingo squares like "has a tattoo" or "speaks a second language," and so on. They could have created mixed site teams for trivia, or other games as well.

Another way to think about making fun as inclusive as possible is to think about specific tasks and needs for the event combined with employees' specific interests. Whether it's an ice cream social, a talent show, an employee art gallery, a winery mixer, or even a Ping-Pong tournament, there are ways to get people involved in planning and support roles. Think about what is needed prior to the event, at the event, and after the event. Perhaps you want to build excitement for the winery mixer with a fun invitation a couple of weeks prior. Lisa in account management loves arts and crafts and can get a crew together to decorate plastic wine glasses and fill them with candy! You'll need a photographer to capture great shots of the talent show, and every office has that one guy with a camera that costs more than his car! Ask your office TikTok star to create some video clips to advertise for the event or capture footage of the festivities. For those who don't want to be in the Ping-Pong tournament, do trivia, or display their talent, have them be judges, advice givers, coaches, or cheer for their favorite team. When the event is done, see who might want to compile the pictures to post on a bulletin board, put in a newsletter, or write a recap for the company blog. There are countless ways to get people involved in the fun, and the more this happens, the more the entire team buys in to the culture.

- **Go organic.** Years ago, I had a boss who was incredibly clean and tidy. I mean, I keep a fairly clean desk, but his office could have been used as an operating room. One day, we had a lunch meeting in his office, and I left the unused mustard packet from my sandwich on his table. I know this because I found it sitting in my office mailbox the next day. Thus began our stupid mustard packet game. I remember finding a mustard packet underneath my computer mouse and I know I taped one to the mouth part of the receiver of his phone. This went on for months and began to include everyone in the office. I remember going to an important meeting with some local government agencies, opening my file folder to grab the agenda, and couldn't help but smile when I saw a damn mustard packet!

  No, the mustard wasn't organic—but the fun was. This type of spontaneous organic fun is just as important and effective as fun that is planned. Researchers from the University of Auckland found that encouraging organic fun helps employees refresh themselves as well as enjoy and engage more with their work.[6] So when you notice employees or colleagues engaging in that random email pun-a-thon or a recycle bin three-point contest, applaud their enthusiasm, and remember participation is even better than permission. Fun in a work setting can be either planned or fanned, so fan the flames of fun when it pops up organically!
- **Surprise! They don't need to know it's coming.** You don't need to send out a Doodle poll to check availability or put a fun

activity on the entire team's calendar a year in advance to reap the rewards of fun. That wonderful pleasure chemical dopamine is triggered with the element of surprise.[7] Don't be afraid to mix things up. The meticulously planned office-to-office ice cream social where each person is responsible for doling out a different topping is one fun way to get people to visit one another in a siloed environment. But for a different team, a surprise visit from an ice cream truck could provide just the boost of joy needed to get through a tough afternoon.

- **Celebrate small wins.** If you're looking for moments or reasons to add a little fun to the day for your team or yourself, look for moments of progress—no matter how small. One of the key ingredients to happiness, and something that boosts emotions and motivation during a workday, is the sense that we're making progress.[8] One way to build a celebration of progress into your work is to gamify your tasks. For yourself, this could mean breaking up a large project into smaller tasks with rewards. After step one is done you get to go grab that latte, after step two, you draw or play the ukulele or shop online for a new puppy, and so on. You can also gamify team tasks with things like leaderboards, badges, increasing levels, and scoring systems with rewards for each. Management and consulting company Deloitte increased the completion time of its leadership training program by 50% with a 47% boost in engagement on its training website after adding gamification elements.[9] Whether it's gamifying work tasks or finding small ways to recognize colleagues for their progress, those mini milestones are a perfect spot to fit in micro-doses of fun. Nice, I just finished writing the section about celebrating small wins . . . I'm gonna go celebrate!
- **Go deep.** Okay, I'm back. It's time to get back to work, and for some people fun at work is directly linked with the work itself. Research suggests that many employees see fun as engaging in their work in a different, more creative, or deeper way.[10] Deep fun might look like bringing in expert panels for your employees to engage with or letting team members design plans for the

new breakroom, conference room, or outdoor plaza that's being built. You could even have a "CEO for a day" brainstorming contest where teams come up with their best solutions and changes to company policies that affect them. Fun is like a swimming pool. Sometimes we need a light refresh by playing catch with a friend in the shallow end, while other times it feels good to dive into the deep end, swim some laps, and get a workout.

If all the details of those fundamentals are too much to remember, Figure 8.1 is your *Fun*damentals of Fun cheat sheet.

The Fundamentals of Fun at Work:

- ✓ Your fun is your responsibility
- ✓ Make it fun for everyone
- ✓ Celebrate small wins
- ✓ Go organic
- ✓ Surprise! (They don't need to know it's coming)
- ✓ Go deep

FIGURE 8.1 The *Fun*damentals of Fun cheat sheet.

As promised, following are 101 ways to have more fun at work. These are just ideas to get you started. Some might be a perfect fit for your work situation and others may not, but feel free to play with them, tweak them, and make them yours! When you choose something to implement, just remember to run the concept through the *Fun*damentals of Fun first!

101 Ways to Have More Fun at Work

Just for You

1. This book! Read this book on a break or try some of the Humor Habits and homework activities in it.
2. Listen to a funny podcast or comedy routine on your commute to and from work rather than news or work-related material.
3. Do something fun with your wardrobe that's just for you. (Think Madeleine Albright and her pins.) Wear some fun socks, that neon 1980s hairclip, or that pair of boxers with ducks on the back that says "Butt Quack." Sound stupid? It's okay, it's your stupid secret!
4. Read your emails to yourself as a funny character or celebrity (think Edna Mode from *The Incredibles* or Seth Rogen from pretty much anything).
5. Post a funny picture of yourself on social media and ask people to caption it for you.
6. Find a picture or something online that you think is funny, reminds you of something funny, or a time when you laughed a lot and set it as your phone or desktop background or screensaver.
7. Try to respond to someone's emails or texts only in Haiku form and see how long it takes them to notice. In case you forgot how to write in haiku form:

   Write five syllables
   then use seven syllables
   then finish with five

   I just explained haiku form in haiku form. Meta!

(You just counted the syllables in each line to double-check my math, didn't you?)

8. Have lunch with or call and talk to your favorite non-work friend.
9. Maintain your own file of funny work stories like customer complaints, funny quotes, goof-ups, and emails.
10. Get physical. Put on some music and go for a quick walk, go up and down the stairs, do some yoga, see how many times you can spin in your chair with one push, anything to get the blood pumping.
11. Change one small thing. Take a different route on your commute, get a different coffee than your usual, add something new to your office, rearrange the furniture, or rearrange your desktop or phone icons to keep things interesting.
12. Gamify your tasks. Whether for the sake of productivity or just to relieve boredom, create games out of your work. See how long you can stand on one foot while completing that online training video or make a work version of an advent calendar with rewards for yourself on key dates or progress markers.
13. Have a "thinking thing." Keep a go-to game, toy, or tinker thing handy to help you get creative, problem-solve, or blow off steam. It could be a dart board, Legos, puzzle cubes, a Nerf basketball hoop, juggling balls, or a drawing pad.
14. Have a funny palette cleanser. Whether you just had a frustrating phone call or meeting, or you're anticipating one, reset your mood with a laugh from one of the funny videos you've been collecting.

Working from Home

15. Do an "anchor commute." As a symbolic transition from home to work mode in the morning, take a 10- to 15-minute walk as your "commute." This will help you refresh your mind and give you a chance to listen to those funny podcasts to start your day like commuters can! Also, every anchor needs to be pulled

up eventually, so transition from work mode back to home mode with another anchor commute at the end of the day.

16. Play a musical instrument for a break or to get creative juices flowing.
17. Play with your dog, kid, or partner for a quick break. Yeah, I said it. Play with your partner. The interpretation is up to you—just make sure you're not still logged onto Zoom.
18. Take a 10-minute weed break. No, not that kind of weed. See how many weeds you can pull out of the yard in 10 minutes. Do that each day for a couple weeks and your yard, weedless to say, will have no needs.
19. Go on a field trip. Change your location from your home office to the backyard, your favorite lunch spot, or that park that's always crowded on weekends but not on Wednesdays.

In Meetings

20. Start the meeting with a quick, light go-around question like: "What is a guilty-pleasure TV show, song, or movie?" of "If you had a superpower in your job what would it be?" or "The weirdest thing you've eaten," and so on.
21. Add funny quotes, jokes, or memes to the meeting agenda.
22. Add a "caption contest" picture or cartoon to the agenda with a prize for the best caption.
23. Play "Buzzword Bingo" during the meeting. Make Bingo cards using overused work phrases that you know will come up and have a prize for who gets Bingo.
24. Have a "Buzzword Buzzer" to avoid overused words or phrases—person with most buzzes brings treats to the next meeting.
25. Name your meeting room based on the culture of your organization and decorate accordingly. Companies like LinkedIn, Bank of America, Politico, Buzzfeed, SpaceX, and Airbnb are doing it, so why shouldn't you join in on the fun?[11]

26. Begin or end your meeting with a funny video. Put a new person in charge of selecting a video for every meeting.
27. Move the meeting location or style just to change it up. Meet outside, on a different floor, in a circle with no desks, or standing up.
28. Warm up: Give a fake word to the group and give a prize for the best definition (you can even have them use it in a sentence).
29. Warm up: Have the team give a fake work announcement or update as a group, but one word at a time going around in a circle. (This helps everyone focus on listening to each other and building on one another's ideas.)
30. Warm up: Have everyone describe how their week is going by what type of car it would be (or animal, or food dish, etc.).
31. Have a "Whine Tasting" section of the agenda where each person gets 20 seconds of uninterrupted and overdramatic whining about a problem of their choice. (See "Exaggeration" section in Chapter 12.)
32. Have the team agree on a funny word or phrase to say when the meeting gets off track and you need to refocus. It can be an inside joke or something that aligns with your culture. The serious folks at *Harvard Business Review* use the example "Jellyfish" as a meeting saver, so I think you're good to get as silly as you want.[12] A prop works well for this too. People get the message as a stuffed cow in a cape is slowly raised in the air.
33. Give your meeting a theme, from the agenda to the way you run it (movie, TV show, sports). You can even have people participate as though their character in the movie would.
34. Play music while you're waiting for people to arrive. You'll notice that turning the music off captures the attention of those who are chatting and signals that the meeting is starting.
35. Add a "soapbox" section to the agenda and pass around a bar of soap for anyone to vent on their "soapbox" about something they need to get off their chest.
36. Ask someone else to run the meeting (bonus if you tell them to do their best impression of you).

37. Give the last person to arrive at the meeting a standing ovation for no reason.
38. Greet everyone at the door with a goofy smile and "high five" with no explanation.
39. Have a "speed meeting" and see how fast you can get through the agenda (use this occasionally to save the team time).
40. Agree that music will play (like at the Oscars) when people's time is up at the end of their department update or presentation.
41. Do fun pop quizzes. Give a prize or candy to anyone who can recite the core values or mission statement or other information about the organization.
42. Download a sound effects app and put someone in charge of doing sound effects for the meeting (clapping, drumroll, buzzer, laughs, etc.).
43. Have cards with trivia, jokes, quotes, or fun questions sitting out for people to interact with while they're waiting for the meeting to begin.

Virtual Meetings

44. Use a team fun and engagement app that works in your virtual meeting platform. *Funtivity* is an example that provides virtual escape rooms, brain teasers, games, and creative challenges. Companies like Zoom and Salesforce use these virtual activities to engage their teams.[13]
45. Have a fun question on the screen or in the chat for people to answer (in the chat or verbally) as they're waiting for all participants to arrive. Make it something different than "Where are you joining from?" like "What was your favorite cartoon growing up?" or "What was your favorite thing to do as a kid?" or "If you could go eat dinner anywhere in the world tonight, where would you go?"
46. Play a round of "Guess the Song." Just go to YouTube and search "Guess the song game" and you'll find free videos where they play a short portion of a song and you have a time limit to

guess it. Videos like this can be shared over your virtual meeting platform so the whole team can play for a fun break.

47. Have a virtual "Cribs" or "Show and Tell" where team members take their laptop or phone, give a tour of their home, or show one thing that is unique or meaningful to them.
48. Do a team video challenge. Divide the group into teams and have them create one-minute videos with prizes for the best, most creative, funniest, and so on. The videos can be just for fun around a holiday theme or they can be work related about creative ways to solve a certain problem or videos portraying the company values. This encourages team members to work together outside of normal meeting times and makes for a fun meeting when everyone gets to watch each other's videos!
49. Play charades. Virtual meeting platforms lend themselves well to games like charades because when you're in person there's always that one guy who yells out the answer when the other team is guessing. On Zoom, you just have the other team muted while the guessing team plays. You can also get thousands of charades clues online by Googling charades generator.
50. Play free virtual games. Google free virtual Family Feud or other popular games and you'll find a variety that you can try out and share with your team virtually.
51. Play "Whose Fridge?" Have each team member send a photo of the inside of their refrigerator. Share all the photos on the screen and see if people can guess whose fridge is whose. This game helps team members get to know each other in a different way and always leads to some laughs.

In the Work Environment

52. Have a contest to name the copy machine or other highly used pieces of office equipment. A county department of health I worked with ended up with names for their copy machine like "The artist formerly known as Prints" (Prince) and "Scandolf" (Gandolf). Not bad!

53. Get a "joke a day" calendar for a common area or your office.
54. Have a "Pun-kin Patch" or a "Winter Pun-derland" with pumpkins or snowflakes on the wall where people write their best puns about work, the holidays, or anything under the pun.
55. Create a funny staff bulletin board with each employee making a funny face and a "fun fact" about them. Or have a bulletin board with pictures of the staff now versus high school or as a baby.
56. Make a "Just for Fun" bulletin board with cartoons, quotes, and funny pictures.
57. Have a "Move to Music" break in the afternoon. One employee picks a song and for the duration of that song people get up, walk around, stretch, dance, or whatever movement is the opposite of what they have been doing. For some jobs it would be a "Sit for a Song" break.
58. Use nationaldaycalendar.com to get ideas to celebrate fun, unusual, and forgotten-about days, weeks, and months of the year! From National Spaghetti Day on January 4 to National Square Dance Month in September, there are literally thousands of ideas from this one resource! Fitting that April is Stress Awareness Month and National Humor Month. Oh, and don't forget Boss's Day on October 16.
59. Put your paper recycle bin on a high shelf or on the wall so you have to make a basket to throw paper away.

Team Engagement

60. Have a game outside of work (kickball, softball, bowling, laser tag, etc.). Divide teams according to your goals—some can cheer on, referee, take photos, or provide snacks.
61. Snowball fight two truths and a lie! The team gets in a circle and each person writes down two true things about themselves and one lie on a white piece of paper then crumples it into a ball. The facilitator yells "Go!" and for 20–30 seconds, you have a snowball fight with all the crumpled paper.

Then each team member picks one up and tries to find the person they think it belongs to.

62. Have the staff cook a gourmet meal together. Divide teams into main course, side dish, appetizers, and dessert. See how well they can follow the recipes and work together!
63. Have a Family Open House where families can come tour the office and meet co-workers.
64. Host a "Staff Olympics." Events could include bowling with plastic bottles and a tennis ball, building a house of cards, or whatever you think your team would enjoy. Have them brainstorm the events or find some online.
65. Create a "Job Switch" day where employees switch jobs with one another to get an idea about other people's positions (this is particularly impactful when the supervisor gets to do some frontline duty).
66. Celebrate people! Not just birthdays, but continuing education, babies, work anniversaries, or any other meaningful personal or professional achievements.
67. Humor Jar! Have an empty jar with slips of paper in a prominent location. Then, when funny things happen, team members write it down and put it in the jar. Depending on how many you have, you can use the funny moments to start or end meetings or have a laugh during tough times.
68. Hold a staff talent show to let people show off. Mike Parra, the CEO of DHL Express U.S., says they have fun with a "DHL's Got Talent!" competition.[14]
69. Have an "All about You" moment. Assign people one day where they get to share a slideshow of pictures about themselves, a favorite vacation, their families, and so on. Put a time limit on the presentation and give a forum for others to ask questions. Depending on team size, the presentations could be done electronically, in meetings, or at a special time at the end of each week.
70. Have a contest to see who can match each employee to their pet.
71. If possible, have a "Bring Your Dog to Work" day.

72. Have a fun photo booth with props at work one day, and give people a break to take funny pictures with each other—then post the pictures on a bulletin board or in the break room. Pair this one with the calendar idea and the photo booth can go with the theme of the day, week, or month.
73. Start a company book or film club.
74. Create an office scavenger hunt. One of the world's largest job and recruiting sites, Glassdoor, uses an office scavenger hunt to make their new employee onboarding program more fun.[15]
75. Have a game of "People Bingo" where the Bingo squares are "find someone who . . ." and they have to get other employees to sign their spot if they speak another language, play a musical instrument, have ever been on TV, and so on.
76. Have people draw or paint with their nondominant hands and then hang them up on the fridge or a bulletin board like children's art.
77. Have a progressive "Mashed-Potini" party. Use an ice cream scoop for mashed potatoes and put them in plastic martini glasses with fun toppings. It's amazing how excited grown adults can get over mashed-potinis. In the heat of the summer, make it a progressive "Sundae on Monday" party with ice cream.
78. Bring as many team members as possible to attend important colleague personal events like graduations, karate tournaments, band gigs, or child births. Wait, not child births. Just wanted to make sure you were still paying attention.
79. Invite former employees or retirees to company events (especially the fun former employees).
80. Have everyone fill out "My Favorites" sheets to be used for holiday gifts or activities like their favorite movie, drink, food, store, music, sports team, hobby, color, etc.
81. Have a game of "Office Chair Curling." Set up a target, then someone has to roll an office chair down a hallway and see how close they can get to the bullseye. Depending on safety, this could be done with someone in the chair as well. Prize for

whoever gets the closest! If people are on different shifts, have them video record their shots!

82. A "Nerfs of Steel" competition. Get some Mega Nerf darts, pool noodles, plastic cups, and eye protection (the funnier the glasses the better). One partner holds their palms out flat with cups in their hand while the other blows the darts through the pool noodle to knock them off. Other roles can be dart runners to bring darts back and forth, people taking video/pics, and others cheering on the winners!
83. Create fun awards to be given out at random or at an awards banquet, but keep them positive and appropriate, such as, Best Laugh, Cleanest Desk, Best Voicemail Voice, and so on.
84. Have staff complete the NCAA Basketball Tournament Brackets and have a trophy for the winner. Each year, engrave the winner's name and they get to keep the trophy at their desk for bragging rights.
85. Do the same as No. 84, but with the Academy Awards. There are templates online to choose your winners in all the categories.
86. Celebrate mistakes! Have an annual "Laugh at Yourself" award given to the person with the best "bad day on the job" story or mistake they made that they can now laugh about.
87. Have "Welcome Parties" for new hires rather than always focusing on "Goodbye Parties" for people leaving.
88. "School Spirit Day!" Have people wear the colors or gear from their favorite schools, whether it's their high school, college, favorite college team, or their kids' school. Tell them to get creative—maybe Carl in accounting, who's an avid angler, will wear a shirt with a school of fish.
89. Crowdsource almost any idea via a contest—a new name for a product, new way to do something, new slogan, and so on. Making it into a contest makes it fun and also gives employees a voice.
90. Celebrate team progress! Whether it's small wins like getting through a busy time of year, or getting next fiscal year's budget approved, or bigger things like the company's anniversary, take

time to celebrate. When eyeglasses company Warby Parker turned five, it hired a marching band and had a parade down the shortest street in New York City. When they reached 1,000 employees, it hung a huge banner outside its building with every employee's name on it in the order they were hired.[16]

In Presentations

91. Find funny pictures or memes that correlate with your topic and put those in the presentation (strategically insert them in places where the content gets dry or the presentation may feel long).
92. Let the audience play "Buzzword Bingo" while you're giving a presentation! If you know there are words or phrases you'll use often, keep them engaged by tracking your jargon on a bingo card—just be ready to have a prize for the winner!
93. Think of the top three funny stories that you tell your friends . . . can you weave one of those into your presentation to highlight a point or make it memorable?
94. Find funny props to compliment your key points.
95. Google funny stories or jokes about your topic to use to break up drier content.
96. Find fun or random trivia facts about your topic and add polls to your presentation or ask for volunteers to try to answer.
97. Use a funny photo of yourself or an old childhood photo to add a little self-enhancing humor to the presentation.

In Emails

98. Make emails more fun with caption contests. Rather than just sending out that same old boring email, include a funny picture or cartoon and ask for the best caption.
99. Make your subject or first line of the email topical to current events: "The Taylor Swift Concert of Sales Updates" or "Pause Your Fantasy Football Draft! It's Time for Quarterly Marketing Numbers."

100. Did you forget the attachment? Google a funny meme about forgetting the attachment (there are tons of them), and paste it in the body of the email when you send it . . . it turns the mistake into a gift!
101. Create a "Monday Madness" or "Friday Funny" email that gets sent out once per week with a funny video.

Humor and laughter seem to pop up spontaneously most of the time, but it's typically when we're having fun. So, if you can't think of any humor or you aren't feeling funny, then look toward fun. Besides, you can't really have funny without it.

Humor Homework

Fun over Funny

Remember, your fun is your responsibility. Do one fun thing just for yourself each day this week at work. You can select one from the "Just for You" or "Working from Home" sections of the 101 ways to have more fun at work, or come up with your own. *(Whether you decide to write haiku emails or recreate a* Star Wars *scene out of paperclips and Legos on your desk . . . it's okay; it will be our little secret!)*

Fun at work just for me this week:

Reflect: What did you notice about micro-dosing a little fun just for yourself?

____

____

____

____

You guessed it, the next assignment is to have fun with other human beings. Choose one *new* way to have fun with your colleagues this week. It doesn't need to be a sneak attack.

You can show them the list or brainstorm your own way. Celebrating a small team win is a great excuse and an easy way to start.

This week for fun, we . . . ________________________

The best, most fun, or funniest part about it was . . .
____
____

By the time we were done, I felt . . . ________________
____
____

9 Tell Your Story

If you've read this much of the book then it probably means that either your sense of humor is an important part of your identity, you'd like your work to be a little more fun, or you're my editor and had no choice (in which case . . . am I using too many of these parenthetical asides? LMK, thx!). If a life with more levity *is* important to you—particularly at work—then it should be part of the story you tell. There should be indications of your affinity for fun and signals inviting humor from others. Most of the tools in Chapter 6 provide strategies for how to send out those signals as an individual, but as an organization, how can you show that you value humor and fun as a part of the organizational culture and identity? A survey of over 700 CEOs across multiple industries found that 98% of CEOs said they prefer candidates with a sense of humor.[1] Of course! We'd all like to work with people with a sense of humor, wouldn't we? In fact, who are those 2% who responded no? I just picture an angry dude who looks like the Monopoly guy, speaks like a 1920s businessman, and owns a pizza delivery restaurant: "Sense of humor you say? That's codswallop! To make and deliver these pies, you just need a sense of smell, sense of taste, and a sense of direction!" as he puts his cigar out on a deep-dish meat lover's supreme. Ideally, we would all get to work with colleagues who know how to laugh at themselves or not succumb to chronic seriousness too often, and that level of humility and lightness might even spread to our toughest clients and customers. As author Simon Sinek often says, "Customers will never love a company unless the employees love it first."[2] If humor is something you value, then how are you attracting those types of employees and customers to your organization or showing them that a little (or a lot, depending on your business) of levity is welcome? Here are some areas where you may be able to make humor a part of your organization's story.

Job Descriptions and Interviews

I'm not just talking about listing "A good sense of humor" or a "Work hard, play hard mentality" in the desired qualifications. In fact, there are a lot of career consultants who are warning job seekers to steer clear of job descriptions with that type of language because it could be a sign that the company expects employees to put up with inappropriate or toxic humor. The key is to do more than just list those things—demonstrate them! Don't put "sense of humor" as a requirement without showing yours. The best way to tell your job applicants that humor is a part of your organization's story is to demonstrate a small glimpse of it. If your business or profession is quite serious, then perhaps it's just one small play on words, or if your industry is very informal and lively then perhaps a little more. The key is to use humor in the job description that is specific and genuine to your industry and even better, your company's culture. Give them a little taste of what it might be like to work with you and your team. Here are a few examples of snippets from job descriptions that use a little humor to help the applicant get a vibe for the humor culture of the organization.

Freedom Trail Realty School, Inc.: Online Real Estate Instructor

> *Our ideal candidate will be:*
>
> - *Tech Savvy.*
> - *Reliable.*
> - *Knowledgeable about real estate and current regulatory and legal concerns.*
> - *Thoughtful about class structure and curriculum design.*
> - *A fan of overusing gifs on Slack.*
> - *No seriously, we use a lot of gifs.*[3]

From those last two bullet points, you can get a sense of the type of humor they're talking about. The added advantage to showing a little bit of your team's specific humor is that it helps you find the right fit. It's possible that a potential applicant reads the job description and is put off because it sounds like too distracting of an environment, not professional enough, or they don't know what a gif is. That person probably wouldn't be a good fit, so if they don't apply then . . . insert your favorite "sorry, not sorry" gif here.

VCA Animal Hospitals (Mars Corp.): Veterinary Technician Internal Medicine

> *. . . we not only work hard, we play hard too. We love a potluck lunch! We practice leaving notes of kindness, go on Starbucks runs, and ice cream magically appears in the freezer from time to time. Our jobs can be stressful, so we expect professionalism while appreciating a good sense of humor. You'll regularly hear knock-knock or "dad" jokes being exchanged in our treatment room.*[4]

This is great. Anyone can say they work hard and play hard, but I'm ready to apply now just for the ice cream, Starbucks, and dad jokes! Here are a few examples from job descriptions that use humor based on the industry or job duties.

Wynn L. White Consulting Engineers: Registered Engineer or Architect

Growing engineering firm looking for a proactive, "batteries-included" engineer or architect to provide hands-on critical thinking skills and building/environmental science . . .

Other assets we're looking for:

- *4+ years engineering or architectural experience and professional registration.*
- *Adaptable and flexible with a sense of humor.*
- *Not afraid to use the telephone as a voice tool.*
- *Detail-oriented planner.*
- *Personable, energetic, and fun to work with.*[5]

The "batteries included" part at the beginning was just so on-brand for an engineer, and then the "not afraid to use the telephone as a voice tool" hit it out of the park!

Laundry Service: Copywriter

Laundry service seeks a quick-witted writer and editor to craft copy for the social channels of our best-in-class clients. You revel in portmanteau. You should swoon over a well-chosen adjective. You think a picture is worth 140 characters, and, boy, do you have opinions on both the Oxford comma AND the em dash. You've been editing this paragraph in your mind as you read it.[6]

I had to look up *portmanteau*. Unless you're a **brainiac**, you'll have to look it up on the **internet** too. Although I could **mansplain** it to you over **brunch** sometime when we're both **hangry** and need to **chillax**.

Brody Brothers Pest Control: Assistant Marketer/ Marketing Coordinator

> *Are you a creative self-starter with a passion for learning and a knack for social media? Are you ready to take your marketing career to the next level? Are you okay with being indirectly implicated in the death of parasites? If so, please read on about this opportunity at our pest control company!*[7]

I feel like whoever wrote these job ads should be their new copywriter and marketing coordinator.

Having a job description that requires humor without using any is like having a job description that requires applicants to have excellent attention to detail with multiple typos. Unless, of course, you're doing it in jest like Level 99 Entertainment did in their job description:

> *We are seeking awesome individuals who demonstrate skills in the following areas to join our Guide Team:*
>
> - *Humor skills.*
> - *Friendliness skills.*
> - *Public speaking skills.*
> - *Problem solving skillls.*
> - *Sense of urgency skills.*
> - *Some tech savviness skills.*
> - *Attention to detail skills. (If you didn't notice that "problem solving skillls" had too many "Ls" then this might not be one of your skills, but we still believe in you.)*[8]

As you can see, there are a ton of ways to tell your story by showing applicants a sneak peek at how you find the funny at work.

Once you have the perfect job description with just the right amount of wit for your work, you'll be flooded with quality applicants that hopefully vibe with your sense of humor. The next step is to see if you vibe with theirs. Again, if most of us would like to work with people with a great sense of humor, then why isn't humor something we intentionally elicit or gauge during interviews? The first step is to follow the recommendations from Chapter 6 and show your prospective new hires that you're professional, but you don't take yourself too seriously. The next step is to have at least one question or conversation starter that opens the door for humor, novelty, or fun. The idea is to make them more comfortable, and the more comfortable the interviewee is, the more they will show you their authentic self. This is a good thing no matter what because their authentic self may be a perfect fit as they show a great balance of serious professional expertise combined with a lighthearted story or anecdote. Or their authentic self may be too silly, the wrong kind of humor, or just inappropriate for your organization.

When I was working at the Culinary Institute of America, we were hiring for a chef instructor who would oversee one of the restaurant courses and help manage one of the student-run restaurants on campus. We had several well-qualified candidates, so I knew we would end up with a quality new hire. I met one of the candidates, who was among the most qualified on paper, in the lobby, and we were chatting prior to his interview with the full committee. I remember making small talk and trying to make him feel comfortable before his big interview. I know we were laughing at one point, and although I'm not sure what about, I know it was something benign (probably Harry-Potter–related, as most people who visited the beautiful Greystone castle campus in Napa thought it reminded them of Hogwarts school). In the interview with the committee, we always asked one question about how they're able to keep things light and fun in a busy and stressful industry. Looking back on it, I'm certainly glad he was feeling comfortable enough to share honestly. He said he and his team would have fun by walking past tables and "crop dusting" them. Five of the six of us on the committee immediately looked down at our evaluations and began vigorously writing as the applicant stood with a smile, still waiting for a laugh. Needless to say, he didn't get a laugh . . . or the job. Oh, and the sixth committee member made some edits to her evaluation after we told her that "crop dusting" meant walking by tables and silently farting.

While he had great answers to industry-specific questions and an impressive résumé, in an interview situation where people typically show the best version of themselves, that was the type of humor he displayed. The answers you get to the "light and fun" questions can bring out applicants' personality and give you insight into how fun it could be to work with them . . . or how quickly after the interview you should wash your hands. To get you started, here are a few interview questions to add some levity to the process and help you assess for a humor fit:

- If you could have a superpower in life, what would it be? How do you think that superpower could apply to this job?
- What is a funny quirk about you that your new colleagues should be aware of? (A unique hobby, ridiculous pet peeve, guilty pleasure, food obsession, etc.)
- How do you think an alien from another planet would approach this job? Or describe this position to an alien from another planet.
- If you could be any animal, which would it be and why? How would that animal approach this job?
- If you could watch one movie or TV series for the rest of your life, what would it be?
- How do you make work fun?
- Tell us about a time when you worked with part of a fun team? What made it fun? How did you balance having fun with being productive?
- If your best friend or sibling were here, what would they tell us about you?
- What's the strangest food you've ever eaten?
- If a song played every time you entered a room, what would you choose?
- If our company were going to get a mascot, what should it be and why?
- What makes you laugh?

By adding a touch of your type of humor to your job descriptions and interviews, you're telling the whole story of your organization and are more likely to find the right kind of funny fit.

Marketing and Social Media

I like visiting national parks, but I never felt the need to follow the National Park Service on Instagram until I saw their Instagram post that read: "If you come across a bear, never push a slower friend down . . . even if you feel the friendship has run its course."[9] The description below the post went on to give general safety tips about being in bear country and included more humor like, "most bears don't want to attack you, they usually want to be left alone. Don't we all?" ". . . use your voice (waving and showing off your opposable thumb means nothing to the bear)," "Climbing a tree is not your best choice. Bears can climb trees. Besides, when was the last time you climbed a tree?" and finally, "Climbing a tree may provoke the bear to chase you. If the former friend you pushed down somehow made it up a tree and is now extending you a hand, there's a good chance you're not getting up that tree. Karma's a bear."

Now that I follow the National Park Service page, I get to see all their funny posts, like the ode to 90s R&B group TLC: "Don't go chasing waterfalls . . . cautiously approach and be careful of slippery conditions. In fact, you may just want to stick to the rivers and lakes that you're used to." When I asked Matt Turner, who leads the National Parks Public Affairs, Social Media Department, about the strategy of harnessing humor for the brand of the National Parks, he said:

> *"Especially for a government agency—which people may think of as being a bit by the book—the use of humor and a bit of friendly sass at times (we're all friends here), has brought in a lot of new followers. We do have a lot of important messages and resources to share with the public. Everything from 'Don't pet the fluffy cows (bison)' to 'Always be aware of your surroundings' to 'How to plan*

for the safest hike' and did I already say 'Don't pet the fluffy cows?' If we can get the message out using some humor, or personality, or grab attention with a nod to pop culture, we often see those posts garner much more engagement and shares. People actually read the entire post, or better yet, make a connection that they'll hopefully remember when they get to a park."

The formula definitely worked on me. The humor sucked me in, and now I also know when to reserve camping spots in the parks, what I can and can't take, and of course, which friend I should bring to bear country (looking at you, Jeremy).

As it turns out, funny marketing doesn't just work on self-proclaimed humor nerds like me. Marketing analytics and strategy company Influential analyzed all the commercials from the 2020 Super Bowl. Specifically, they were looking to see which ads delivered the highest amount of purchase intent from users. The top 5 ads with the highest amount of consumer purchase intent were humorous ads, as well as 9 of the top ten.[10] When I asked Influential's Vice President Talin Koutnouyan about the study, she said the data from over 12 million consumer mentions of the ads were clear and that "humor helps 'Trojan horse' initiatives into the mind." (I didn't know Trojan horse could be used as a verb, but I think I like it!)

It can be scary and daunting to use humor in marketing or social media, but it could be worth the dividends. According to the 2022 Oracle Humor and Happiness Global Research Study that includes data from over 12,000 consumers and 3,100 business leaders across 13 countries:[11]

- 91% of consumers said they prefer brands to be funny and 90% are more likely to remember funny ads, yet business leaders said that only 20% of their offline ads and 18% of online advertising actively used humor.
- 75% of people say they would follow a brand if it is funny on social media, yet only 15% said their brand is humorous on social media.

- 69% of people say they would open an email from a brand if the subject line were funny, but only 24% of business leaders say they use humor in their email marketing.
- If a brand uses humor, 80% of consumers said they would buy from that brand again and recommend it to family and friends, while 72% would choose that brand over the competition.
- Finally, despite all of the preceding data, 95% of business leaders fear using humor in customer interactions, and 85% don't believe they have the tools or data necessary to do so.

If you skipped or just skimmed over all those stats, I don't blame you. Here's a visual summary:

Consumers want brands to be funny.

Another agency that used humor in marketing was the office of the U.S. president. When the Obama administration first tried to roll out the healthcare.gov site for Obamacare and it crashed, making the initial rollout skid to a halt, they went to a professional to help them rebound from the embarrassment—comedian Zach Galifianakis. Once the website was fixed, Obama made an appearance on Galifianakis's YouTube show *Between Two Ferns,* which got millions of views, where he was able to drive viewers to the new and improved website.[12]

Even The American Heart Association was able to use humor to raise awareness about heart disease being the No. 1 killer of American women with their video "Just a Little Heart Attack."[13] Comedic actress Elizabeth Banks humorously tries to be the perfect mom while denying that she's having a heart attack and "Trojan horsing" (you had to know that was coming) important information about heart disease in the minds of the viewers.

Auto Responses, Chatbots, and Websites

Living in a digital age, a lot of our online communication is with AI bots and programmed responses rather than real people. The good thing is that (at least for the time being) we still control the robots! You can give your website, automatic email responses, chatbots, and even unsubscribe email pages a human-like quality with a touch of humor. While it's still obvious that you're dealing with a bot when using the chat feature on company websites, most consumers would rather chat with a fun bot over a boring bot. Sixty-eight percent of people said they would prefer to engage with a chatbot/digital assistant that's funny, yet only 27% of business leaders said their brands incorporate humor into bot communications. So, if their company's bot is humorless, and humans programmed it, then who are the real robots?

Leave it to a company like National Geographic to bravely explore the vast world of bots with a touch of humor. As their new series about the life of Albert Einstein was getting set to premiere, they rolled out an Einstein chatbot on Facebook that would interact with users' messages and questions in the voice of the legendary brainiac (there's one of those portmanteaus again). He opens the conversation plugging his new show and randomly ends with, "Socks are optional." When asked to explain, he states that he's, "reached an age that when someone tells me to wear socks, I don't have to." When a user asked how the Einstein bot was doing, he replied, "If you consider the fact that the universe is accelerating infinitely into nothingness, I'd have to agree . . . things are indeed going relatively well, aren't they?"[14]

Companies like Bark Box, Charity Water, Groupon, and Sidekick all use humor in their "unsubscribe from email" pages.[15] While people still may choose to no longer receive emails from them, at least they're leaving with a final dose of fun and increasing the chances that they're leaving with a positive experience from the brand. When you unsubscribe from Groupon, it shows you a gif of a guy named Derrik and blames him for being the one who thought you would like those emails. Sidekick reaches out to people who haven't opened their content in a long time, explaining that it doesn't want to be that annoying unread email in your inbox and offering to unsubscribe for you, while Bark Box, of course, has a picture of a cute dog trying to talk you into staying. Charity Water leaves you with a video of its CEO getting doused with water at his desk. Leaving customers with a laugh when they unsubscribe from emails is brilliant. I mean, if someone's breaking up with you, you might as well leave them with a reminder of how witty and funny you are (I'm talking to you, Meghan from seventh grade).

Your brand doesn't have to be funny, and you don't need to overuse humor or be obnoxious about it. Dollar Shave Club does a good job of injecting a subtle amount of humor on its website. In the product description for its small black travel toiletries bag (an objectively unfunny product), they throw in a tiny bit of humor in the list of features: ". . . magnetic closure, open-top construction, hand-woven paracord opener, doesn't hold your emotional baggage."[16] Even if you don't sell products directly on your website, there are excellent opportunities to show a little personality on your "about us" pages by having more fun photos and facts about the staff, or on your frequently asked questions pages, and even newsletter sign-up forms. Sure, the website response when a form is completed can read, "We received your submission" or "Success," but it just feels more fun and human if it says, "Boom, got it!," or "You did it! Check that off your to-do list!"

At the Office

Social media, websites, and chatbots are great places to make humor a part of your company's story, but as of the release of this book, believe it or not, there is still work that happens not in cyberspace, but in a physical space. If you're lucky enough to get to experience work in an actual building with real-life human beings, then don't forget about adding humor to the physical office space. At the Culinary Institute of America, after a remodel, we needed new "Employees Must Wash Hands" signs for the bathrooms, and I was the person lucky enough to be honored with the task of ordering these signs. When I looked online, however, I came across a photo of a much better sign and decided to make my own. I ended up donning each bathroom with a sign that had a photo of Hans Solo from Star Wars that read "Wash Your Hans." Our institution and the industry are pretty formal, so it's not like we were able to be over the top with humor or silliness, but it was clear that the staff and students enjoyed the little dose of levity on their bathroom break as they would often chuckle and asked who made the signs. One day, I noticed that one of the signs had been written on and I was initially bummed until I got closer to see what it said. In small red ink, just below "Wash Your Hans," it read ". . . or else you'll be flying Solo." That's not bathroom graffiti, that's employee engagement!

From pictures of employees on vacations or with their pets, to fun wall art, or funny signs, you can choose to go all in on humor in the office if that's on brand or be subtle and sophisticated about it if that's the industry standard. Madelyne Cromwell, owner of Cromwell Tax and Bookkeeping, runs a serious financial firm in Santa Rosa, California. On the company's website it mentions how much it *"LOVES tax preparation,"* which makes the company a bit nerdy. The office is clean, quiet, and professional—exactly how you would want your tax expert's space to feel. I get a little anxious with money and numbers due to the trauma of dropping and retaking math four times in college (or was it five?), so I remember feeling a bit on edge walking in and waiting for my tax preparation meeting. Then I finally noticed the quotes that were inconspicuously blending in as wall art in beautiful metallic and glass frames:

"We have what it takes to take what you have.

—Suggested IRS motto"

"Few of us ever test our powers of deduction, except when filling out an income tax form.

—Laurence J. Peter"

"Isn't it appropriate that the month of taxes begins with April Fools' Day and ends with cries of 'May Day'?

—Rob Knauerhase"

"I'm proud to pay taxes in the United States; the only thing is I could be just as proud for half the money.

—Arthur Godfrey"

"The hardest thing in the world to understand is the income tax.

—Albert Einstein"

In a perfectly professional and conservatively decorated accounting office, the subtle humor touch made me realize these were just the number nerds I needed.

Ellie Mental Health: A Case Study in Making Humor a Part of Its Story

Combining several of the strategies provided in this section, Ellie Mental Health is a shining example of how to weave humor into your organization's story on your way to success. Ellie's Founder and CEO, Erin Pash, started the company as one small clinic in Minnesota in 2015. Its refreshing, authentic, and humorous approach to serious work has led it to become the fastest growing (and soon to be the largest) mental health company in the United States. One way Ellie has made humor a part of its story is by explicitly stating it as one of its core values on its website: "Humor. We believe a good sense of humor is an invaluable personality characteristic. We use humor as a therapeutic technique for helping others to see problems in a new light, and as a means of cultivating a welcoming and playful environment for our staff and clients." From LinkedIn and Zappos to AES and Workday, there are many companies that specifically list something like "fun" or "humor" in their core values, which is a great start, but the most crucial step is living those values.

When I asked Pash how Ellie Mental Health lives its value of humor, she told me that they encourage therapists to use humor when appropriate with clients and to embrace the mantra that "Life is hard, so you might as well also make it funny." Ellie makes it clear to potential clients that humor is a part of its story with its irreverent and fun marketing, including a huge billboard that reads "Freaking the %&$# Out?" (Figure 9.1) and with the "merch" it sells online. That's right. Not only can you look for your next therapist on Ellie's website, you can also look for your next outfit! They have T-shirts, hats, and other items designed to destigmatize mental health with humorous quips like "Hold on . . . let me overthink this," "My therapist knows what you did," "My amygdala makes me anxious," and "Everybody sucks sometimes." Finally, if you do want to apply for a job at Ellie Mental Health, you'll immediately know this isn't just any ordinary company when you apply to be its next "Super Awesome Therapist Unicorn."

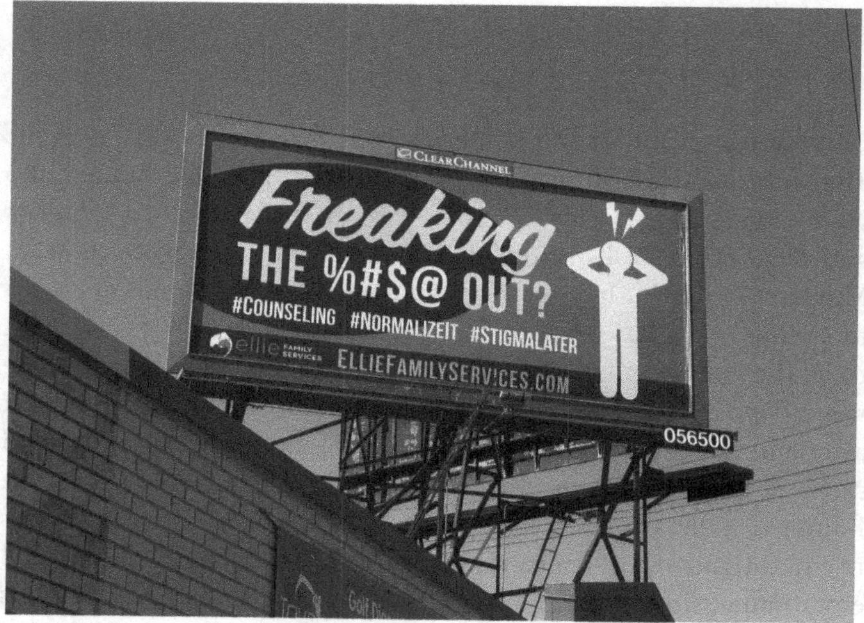

FIGURE 9.1 Ellie billboard. (Credit: Erin Pash)

Making your brand of humor a part of your organization's story not only helps you attract the right type of customers and the right fit for employees, but it can also help your company take off the way Ellie Mental Health has. Depending on your organization, humor may fit more naturally into the culture like in interviews and job descriptions, but not so much in the marketing and social media realms. Perhaps it's important to keep your physical space serious, but there's room for a few LOLs on your website. Whatever industry you're in, your primary consumers are human beings. From moment to moment, human beings naturally flow through emotions of happiness, anger, excitement, and laughter. If you aren't telling the story of your organization with a little humor, you're leaving out a basic element of the human experience.

Humor Homework

Tell Your Story

Find one area where your organization could inject a little humor or levity in their branding or public relations and write down how you might "punch it up" with a little humor if you were in charge. Remember to look at areas like job descriptions, interviews, social media and marketing, websites, and the physical office space. If you work for yourself, you're not off the hook. Can you add a little humor to your LinkedIn bio or promotional materials?

My company's original material:

____

____

____

Telling the same story with some humor:

____

____

____

If you think the leaders in your organization would be open to it, share your idea for the punched-up version with them! If not, just read it to yourself and laugh like an evil movie villain. Now, keep it in a safe place for when you take over the world.

10 Earn It

My freshman year of college I was dripping with self confidence that I can only describe as unwarranted. At 5′4″, 120 pounds, and a solid 6 out of 10 in the looks department, I was the perfect nonthreatening "friend zone" guy for the ladies—but, hey, at least I was also on the fast track to becoming a *C*-average student with a liberal arts degree. That confidence, sense of humor, and little-guy charm had worked wonders for me in high school. Don't get me wrong, I was still in the friend zone with the ladies—but also with the teachers. My good grades in high school were probably 70% charm, 20% smarts, and 10% hard work (it still counts as hard work if it was done during passing periods).

It only took until the first day in my first college class for me to realize college would be different. It was a Philosophy 101 class with about 50 other students in it. I sat in the front row, mostly because I couldn't see and didn't know yet that I'd soon need glasses (another checked box for the friend zone). The professor was a short guy who was somewhere between 45 and 80 years old—it was tough to tell because he had a big, bushy, gray beard, and looked like the perfect caricature of a philosophy professor. He had a booming voice and his first words to the class that echoed off the back walls were, "What . . . is . . . philosophy?" We thought he may go on to tell us the answer, so everyone stayed quiet—but he didn't. He began scanning the room, bugging out his eyes, and raising his eyebrows that matched his bushy, gray beard. He wanted an answer, and I wasn't going to leave him hanging. I raised my hand and before he could even acknowledge me, I started talking: "Philosophy is just a bunch of old white guys worrying about things that nobody understands, and that don't really matter." I got a laugh from my peers, which always feels good, but wasn't the primary goal. I was hoping Professor gray beard would find it amusing. I guess in my head, he would chuckle and give me a "Oh, you . . . good one!" kind of look and the entire semester would be filled with our witty back-and-forth banter culminating in him giving me an *A+* and telling me I was really the smartest student he's ever taught.

Yeah, that didn't happen. Instead, he was quiet for what seemed like an hour and slowly walked over, stared at me, and asked, "Do you not understand because it doesn't matter? Or does it not matter because you don't understand?" I started to reply, but before my mouth sounds made an actual word, he interrupted and said, "You can leave my class until you have a serious answer, and that won't be today." Daaaamn! I finally found a teacher my same height and he just dunked on me in front of the whole class. I learned two valuable things from that interaction. First, **the freedom to use humor with others must be earned**. Second, to be a smart-ass, you must first be smart.

Earn It by Building Trust

If my professor and I had known each other for a long time and had shared laughs about philosophy before, there would be a level of trust between us and then *maybe* he would have found my comment amusing. Just like the way we build trust with people for anything else, the trust to play and use humor with others is built through small actions over time. You may be wondering, "Wait, Paul. Earlier in the book you said humor builds trust, but now you're saying we must have trust to use humor? Which is it?" Wow, you're really paying attention! So, will someone trust you because you make them laugh or do you make them laugh because they trust you? Now I'm having philosophy class flashbacks. The answer is both. When we show others that we can joke with them in a positive, nonthreatening, and inclusive way, we gain their trust to do so more often, and the freedom to play with more types of humor. Some people are chronically serious, and others have been hurt by humor used as a weapon so they're naturally more protective and guarded, but small doses of positive humor will still build trust over time. That trust leads to a feeling of psychological safety where people begin to feel they can let their defenses down a little and be themselves.

For example, I'm very guarded about trusting people with my dogs. I won't let just anyone watch my dogs when I'm out of town. I will, however, let a new neighbor pet my dogs. Then I see them saying hello to the dogs as they pass by, playing with them when they come visit, take a surprise lick to the face in stride, and eventually, they're texting me photos of themselves cuddled in bed together while they're watching my house and I'm on vacation. Show people small doses of positive humor, and before you know it, they'll be licking your face and sleeping with you. Not exactly how I planned that metaphor to work out, but you get the point. So, if we don't have any humor trust built up with someone yet, then what's the safest way to start? The best way to use humor with strangers or in professional settings is to begin with the lowest risk material that takes the least amount of skill and practice required—humor about yourself or your own experience (Figure 10.1).

Initially, sticking to humor about yourself or your own experience decreases your chance of alienating or offending others and increases your chance of using it effectively. It doesn't take as much skill or practice because it's your own story or experience, so chances are you'll deliver the anecdote or joke well. Even if you do flub the delivery, the risk is much lower because you're the topic of the humor. Once you've built up some credibility and trust with your colleagues and/or have been practicing using humor more frequently, then

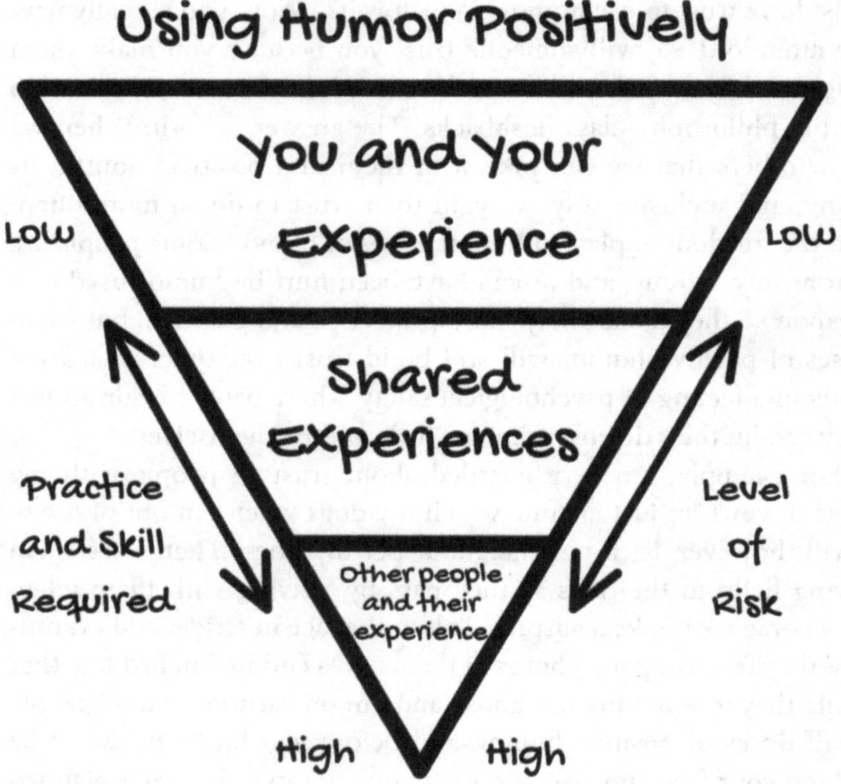

FIGURE 10.1 Using humor positively.

joking about shared experiences is a great way to enhance bonds and connection within the group. Looking back at my comment about philosophy, not only did my professor and I not have a prior relationship of trust between us, but I was also not a member of the group I was making a joke about. He spent his entire career studying philosophy, so it makes sense that he would be upset at an 18-year-old student making fun of his profession. Perhaps if an esteemed philosophy colleague were to joke about them being old men who just argue over things that don't matter, my professor would have taken it in stride or even added a "Yes, and . . ." to his comments and provided his own take. My freshman funny fail happened because

I jumped right to the bottom of the inverted pyramid in Figure 10.1 and tried to use humor about other people and their experiences. It is possible to use humor positively and effectively that is focused on others, but it takes the most practice and skill to deliver and comes with the highest risk of failure. I incurred a high risk and greatly overestimated my own skills to read my audience and deliver effectively. Like I said in the beginning, I was dripping with unwarranted confidence. I was allowed back to class on the second day and went on to earn a *C*, which seems fitting. If I had the first day of class to do over again, I'm sure I would have still tried to use a little humor when the professor asked, "What is philosophy?" What I could have said was . . .

"All I know, is that I know nothing."

—*Socrates.*[1]

When discussing the risks and boundaries of humor, it's imperative to delineate between two different types. Humor that is used daily between friends, family members, colleagues, and even in business marketing is what I classify as "everyday humor." Humor that is specifically written and performed for entertainment purposes like stand-up, improv, movies, TV, books, and so on is "artistic humor."

Humor artists will push the boundaries of popular culture, politics, religion, and all aspects of society just as more "serious" artists like actors, musicians, novelists, playwrights, and painters have done for centuries. So, when it comes to artistic humor, I believe comedians should go for it. Play in the high-risk playgrounds, cross some lines, and occasionally make people uncomfortable because that's sometimes how progress is made, or new forms of comedy are created. Ultimately, if people are offended or turned off by a certain comedian or show, they'll stop paying to see them. The art form both pushes and learns from society at the same time. It's like when Coca-Cola came up with New Coke in the 1980s. As a society, we were all about weird new stuff like Gremlins and slap bracelets, but New Coke was just too far. It got booed off stage never to be seen again.

But chances are you're not a comedian and you're not reading this book to use humor on stage. This book focuses on the everyday humor we use with one another. The use of everyday humor shouldn't be viewed or treated any different than any other form of communication we use with each other. When we interact with one another at work, at home, or at the grocery store, shouldn't we do so with an ethic of care? Ideally, shouldn't our intentions be to lift each other up or at the very least to do no harm? Any time we communicate with other people, we should aim to do so with positive intentions and not to exclude, mistreat, or marginalize them, whether we're using humor or not. This doesn't mean all your humor has to be dad puns and squeaky-clean knock-knock jokes. It is possible to put a smile on your friends' face with a joke about her lack of relationship success or make your boss laugh by joking about his ugly cat, but it only works if you begin with the prerequisite to positive humor.

The prerequisite to positive humor is empathy. Your friend may typically laugh at those relationship jokes, but maybe not after she just had a breakup. Your boss may love a good joke about his ugly cat, but perhaps not after he just put his other one down. When two people laugh together, it's because they have a shared understanding or experience. Shared laughter is empathy in action. When only one is laughing, empathy is lacking.

Take, for example, a *Newsweek* story about a manager who thought telling his employee "You're fired" on April Fools' Day was a funny joke. Unsurprisingly, it completely backfired. A Reddit user shared his experience online about his boss's prank, and that he and other employees didn't find it funny. He packed his office, went home, and his boss called him to tell him it was just a joke. The employee was upset and posted about it online. When the post went viral the employee ended up with his job back, a raise, and a new boss because the jokester was terminated.[2] Ultimately, this is a wildly juvenile joke in the first place, but the lack of empathy is what sticks out. This happened just at the end of the pandemic when people were extremely stressed and many actually were losing their jobs. If the manager had any empathy and gave a thought to how the employees might feel with a joke like that, perhaps he would have chosen not to do an April Fools' Day prank that year. Whether you're trying to make your friends laugh, get a giggle in a meeting, or create a funny social media campaign, it's crucial to start with the prerequisite of empathy. To ensure your humor is coming from an empathetic place, first ask yourself: "Am I trying to *get* a laugh, or *give* a laugh?" Then, it's all about pairing the amount of trust you have with the person with the right type of humor (edgy vs. safe). Figure 10.2 is a guide for when to get edgy or stay safe.

FIGURE 10.2 Humor trust continuum.

It's okay to push the boundaries and take risks with humor, but be aware that the humor rules are different for Margaret Cho than for a CEO.

Meeting Deadlines > Writing Punchlines

Another way to earn the privilege of using humor, particularly in professional settings, is to simply get your shit done and do it well. If you're reliable, you work hard, and produce quality work, then it's much more likely that your humor will be a welcome reprieve than an unwanted distraction. In fact, when it comes to leadership, work ethic and humor are inextricably linked. In a survey of over 2,700 employees across a variety of industries, when employees were asked to describe the most important traits of the best leaders they've worked for, "work ethic" and "sense of humor" are mentioned twice as much as any other characteristic.[3] It's incredible that those two phrases are both mentioned twice as much as any other trait, but as big of a humor nerd as I am, I still believe the work ethic must come first. Nobody wants to see the colleague who never responds to phone calls or emails at every Taco Tuesday happy hour. You can't prioritize punchlines over deadlines.

At work, your best ability is your reliability and without that, it doesn't matter how funny you are. Even if you're great at your job, part of the work ethic and reliability factor is also knowing when your humor is a source of traction versus distraction. When I was younger, as someone who loved to talk and was almost always looking to *get* a laugh, this took me some time to figure out. I was a resident assistant in college, and it was my first "real job." I mean, it included movie nights, the occasional dunk tank, and whip cream pie fights, but I had to go to meetings and not lose keys to the building too, so it was pretty legit. I remember after one of our staff meetings, my boss Dan asked me to stay and talk for a minute. This didn't worry me at all because Dan and I got along great. Although he was

10 years older than me (which when you're 19 feels like a dad), Dan really got my sense of humor and we're still friends to this day. That's why it surprised me when he told me I needed to chill out with all the side comments and jokes in our staff meetings. He said he was trying to explain something, and I was busy being "fun boy" in the corner goofing off and cracking jokes. I told him not to worry because I got everything he was saying, I showed him my notes, and even summarized what he was saying back to him. What he told me after that has stuck with me for the past 28 years (I may have just revealed my age to anyone who can do math). He said, "I'm not worried about you getting the information, I'm worried about you preventing others from getting it." Sadly, I had never even considered that. Come to think of it, this might be what my third-grade teacher was trying to tell me when she said I had diarrhea of the mouth.

Throughout my career, I've tried to become more aware of the nuances of when to use humor and when to hold back, when to pop into a friend's office for a laugh and when to let them work. I haven't always been perfect at it, but it gets easier and easier to read the moment over time. Like any other "soft skill," it's something that takes some practice and self-awareness to refine, but if "fun boy" with diarrhea of the mouth can do it, then so can you. Just ask yourself "Am I trying to get a laugh or give a laugh?" and "Is my humor providing traction or distraction?" You can also ask a trusted colleague or mentor to give you feedback and let you know if your humor is too much, too little, or you're Goldi-Laughs (just right). Ultimately, if you prioritize your work performance and not your comedy performance, your colleagues will come to appreciate, and, hopefully, emulate your levity.

Earn It by Creating Psychological Safety

One of the tallest hurdles to overcome as someone who speaks and consults about humor is the concern from organizational leaders that humor is a slippery slope and can result in inappropriate jokes and hurtful comments. To that concern I say . . . yes, *and* . . . Yes, some people use humor inappropriately or tell jokes that are insensitive or even offensive. *And* . . . it is also quite common that the inappropriate action or comment was not actually intended in jest, and that humor is getting the retroactive blame. "I was just joking" is typically what follows a regrettable action or when someone is caught being offensive, derogatory, or just mean. When Cindy gets upset because she walked by Dave's office and overheard him telling someone "Cindy is so annoying! She keeps coming and asking me questions about the new software system. I'm like, just leave me alone!" Chances are, when asked about it, Dave will say "I was just joking." Either Dave doesn't understand what jokes are, or he just doesn't want to admit he was talking crap about Cindy behind her back.

The real slippery slope isn't humor, it's allowing the toxic behaviors of mistreatment, alienation, intimidation, and harassment to occur without consequence. Your team's humor will match your organization's culture. Remember, humor is life's sweetener, not the main ingredient. The main ingredients in any organization begin with values and behaviors. If dismissive attitudes, intimidating language and tones, hurtful comments, gossip, and antagonistic behaviors are pervasive in an individual or the team, then why would it be any different when they use humor? The best thing you can do to create the psychological safety required for people to have fun and use humor in a constructive way is to address those negative behaviors whether they're humor-related or not. When incivility goes unchecked, it emboldens the callous. Conversely, once a positive, supportive, and inclusive culture is established, most of the levity will mirror the culture.

It's true that humor itself is often not the culprit of the misdeed, but the scapegoat. That being said, there may be times when you're genuinely trying to be funny or use humor and you step in it and say something hurtful or even offensive (Figure 10.3). Of course, if you follow the previous guidelines and proceed with positive intentions, seek to give a laugh, and begin with empathy, then your chances of

Funny Fails:

When you have a humor #*%& up

Remember:

Impact > Intentions

If you have to say "it was just a joke"

then you haven't told one.

The words you're looking for are

"I apologize"

FIGURE 10.3 What to do if your humor harms?

success are greater, but you could still have a funny fail. What do you do if your intentions were good but you unintentionally offend or harm someone?

While there's no guarantee that your relationship will survive a funny fail, a sincere apology plus previous trust, combined with future positive actions and a willingness to learn, is a pretty good recipe for success. John Anderson is an anchor on ESPN's Sports Center and has been on ESPN for over 25 years. His job is to provide commentary on the major sports highlights of the day, and if you've ever watched ESPN, it's known for its entertaining, high-energy, and funny style of delivering the highlights. In May 2023, Anderson was highlighting a game-winning goal from hockey defenseman Zach Whitecloud and said, "What kind of name is Whitecloud? A great name if you're a toilet paper." What Anderson didn't know is that Zach Whitecloud is the first member of the Sioux Valley Dakota Nation to play in the NHL, and he was understandably very upset by the comment. Rather than hiding behind "It was just a joke," Anderson owned his mistake and stated, "This is totally on me and I sincerely apologize to Zach, the Golden Knights, their fans and everyone else for what I said. It's my job to be prepared and know the backgrounds of the players and I blew it."[4] I would argue that even if Whitecloud wasn't a member of the Sioux Valley Dakota Nation, the comment was still ill-advised. Most people, regardless of their background, probably, don't want their last name compared to toilet paper, but the cultural significance definitely adds more gravity to the misstep. The respect Anderson had earned over his career combined with an apology taking accountability for his actions was enough for the network and for Whitecloud to move forward. Whitecloud told reporters, "I think it was an attempt at humor that came out as being obviously insensitive, and he acknowledges that. He understands that it was wrong to say. I wanted to make sure he knew that I accepted his apology. People make mistakes, and this is a scenario where not just John but everyone can learn from and move forward in a positive direction and try to be better."

It really isn't that difficult to have fun, enjoy work, and use humor without being inappropriate and I call BS on those who claim it's a huge mystery. I guess I just don't see much difference in using humor than using any other form of communication. We generally know when what we're saying is right versus wrong, good versus bad, or helpful versus hurtful. So, for your colleague who still claims they don't know if their brand of humor is appropriate or not, here's a simple guide:

Four signs your workplace humor is inappropriate:

1. You use disclaimers like "I'm not sexist or anything but . . . ."
2. You look over your shoulder or close the door before telling a joke.

3. People's reaction include "Anyways . . ." (trying to quickly change the subject), their laughs turn to groans, it gets quiet, or people look like they want to hide.
4. You often say "It was just a joke," "Where's your sense of humor?," "Lighten up," or "You're too sensitive."

When we live our lives being generally positive, uplifting, and inclusive of others, then our humor will mostly follow suit. It also takes the pressure off being funny. A joke that's inclusive and positive but not funny is, at worst, just confusing.

Humor Homework

Earn It

Be a great colleague by doing at least one of these things:

- Get started on that work thing you're procrastinating.
- Help out a colleague with a project.
- Check in on a colleague to see how they're doing and really listen to them.
- Respond to those phone calls and emails you're dreading to return.

Remember, deadlines > punchlines.

11 Rituals

My friend Chris has two sons, and the boys have a ritual after dinner and before bedtime each night. They take their G.I. Joes in the bathroom and play until they poop—the kids, not the G.I. Joes. First, I know that's a little too much information. Second, no, I am not recommending this as a workplace fun activity. You'll notice it was not on the 101 ways to have fun at work list. I bring it up because rituals are important. Think about a unique ritual your family has or had when you were growing up. It could be a nightly bedtime story, a weekly family dinner or game, or a particular tradition on a holiday. What significance did that ritual have for you and the family? What would happen if you stopped doing it? I often ask this question when facilitating workshops and comments from participants consistently echo research that their rituals provide meaning, structure, comfort, safety, something to look forward to, and help them stay present in the moment or enhance their experience. Chris told me that the play-and-poop ritual started as a way to alleviate anxiety for one of his boys who was having a tough time in that department. Just as my workshop participants shared, this ritual provided structure and safety for Chris's kids and, well, it even enhanced their performance.

It turns out that rituals at work, even if silly or fun like doing the Walmart cheer or shooting a nerf toy gun to conclude a project, enhance performance as well. Employees who participate in regular rituals like these report a 16% increase in how meaningful they find their work and tend to show better "organizational citizenship," like going above and beyond or staying late to help a colleague.[1] Workplace ritual researcher and Harvard Business School professor Michael Norton explains, "It's not that we do rituals and then, magically, we like doing our work later that day, it's that over time, rituals themselves become meaningful to us—a sense of 'this is how we do things around here.' And that meaning is then linked to finding more meaning in the work that we do."[2] Finding meaning in your job sounds fluffy and nice like puppy dogs and rainbows, but productivity is what really counts, right? Right! And employees who find more meaning in their work are more productive, more motivated, and happier—so fun rituals for the win![3] Meanwhile, some employees think things like fun rituals are ridiculous. But guess what? It doesn't matter! The ritual even starts to mean something to the workers who think it's silly, and they begin to feel differently about their co-workers and their work.[4] So puppy dogs, rainbows, and rituals it is!

Like a filet mignon and a fine cabernet, this chapter pairs well with Chapter 8, "Fun over Funny." Now that you have plenty of ideas for humor and fun that can be implemented at work, it's important to think about how to optimize your amusement. Most of the time when a leader or team decides they want more fun at work, they simply pick a random activity, do it, and have a good time. There's nothing wrong with that, but if humor and fun are just haphazard happenings at random times, then it can be difficult to really affect the overall culture. Most organizations spend a fortune on one or two big "fun" events per year like a holiday party or a summer barbeque. Large fun events are awesome and give employees something to look forward to, but alone they don't make much of a dent in creating a culture of fun. You can keep the large events and the small random moments of fun that are working for you, but it's also important to ritualize some of your humor and fun at work. Just like the family rituals that people share with me in workshops, the rituals at work can be daily, weekly, monthly, or annually (Figure 11.1).

Another reason to create consistency with fun and humor at work is because it follows the science of happiness. As you learned in previous chapters, when you laugh or have fun at work, the cocktail of feel-good endorphins flood your brain and it gives you a boost of happiness. If we're doing this at work sporadically or even just a couple of times per year, it will have almost zero effect on the overall happiness of the team. According to happiness expert Shawn Achor, we all have a genetic happiness set point, and when we get our boosts

FIGURE 11.1 Rituals.

of happiness they typically last for a short period of time and then we fall back to our set point. That is, unless we are consistently practicing happiness strategies, in which case, we can slowly over time increase our happiness set point.[5]

This is why you could work at a company where there is the occasional random fun event, but overall, it doesn't seem like a fun place to work. It would be much easier if we could go big on fun once a year and have it last. In fact, I wish we could do it with house cleaning and exercise as well, but just like culture they take consistency. Culture is like water to a fish. It's there every day and almost goes unnoticed. If your culture is chronically serious or even negative, then just one random big fun event may even feel out of place—like someone poured a cup of oat milk into your fishbowl.

In this book, you already have a number of humor habits, interventions, and ways to incorporate more fun at work that you can turn into rituals for you and your team. Additionally, I'll provide a few examples of daily, weekly, monthly, annual rituals in this section to spark your creativity. However, the best place to start developing rituals is by formalizing or enhancing what you and your colleagues already do. It's likely there are already rituals, and you may be able to enhance the experience by calling attention to them, giving them names, providing resources, or including others. A couple of my colleagues at the university and I walked to a nearby local favorite burrito restaurant on half-price burrito Tuesday. Before we knew it, the Tuesday lunch crew began to grow and eventually the entire office was going. It wasn't intentional on our part, but it was clear that in a high-stress job, the midday break was essential for our staff. It was about more than lunch. It was about all the laughs and comradery that happened on the 15-minute walk to the burrito shop. It was a simple thing that became important to us, and it always felt like a shame if we weren't able to go to our Tuesday lunch for some reason. One way we formalized the ritual was that for this one day, we tried to be mindful about leaving enough time between appointments around the Tuesday lunch hour and arranged staff schedules to have a slightly longer lunch break that day of the week. We couldn't completely close the office during lunch, so we had the staff create a rotation of who would stay back each week. Eventually other departments on campus knew we would go get burritos on Tuesdays, and we began to invite campus partner "guests" to our lunches—it was a whole vibe.

Whether it's a healthy sales competition that starts between a few employees, puns shared back and forth via email, or people filling out brackets for the NCAA basketball championships, when you notice humor and fun happening organically, you can solidify it as part of the culture by making the activities inclusive of everyone, providing time and resources to them, and legitimizing them with a proper name, event, trophy, or spot on the meeting agenda. Here are some examples of rituals to get you thinking:

Daily Rituals

Reverse trick-or-treating. One leader from a financial tech company I worked with did reverse trick-or-treating every afternoon. When she felt herself get tired or losing productivity, she would take a break and walk to co-workers' offices to disperse candy.

Afternoon music recharge. Pick a time in the afternoon that always seems to drag and have an entire office break for the duration of one song. People can dance if they want, but don't have to. The only rule during the song is that you must take a break and move around either dancing, walking, stretching, or shaking out the stress of the day. A different employee gets to choose the song each time.

Pun or joke of the day. In a breakroom or prominent staff location, have a funny quote, joke, or pun each day. Ask people to submit suggestions to keep everyone engaged and keep the content fresh.

Weekly Rituals

Wacky Sock Wednesday. Encourage people to wear fun, weird, or wacky socks on Wednesdays. A hospital I worked with started it and found that employees got so into it, they created a Wacky Sock parade on Wednesdays where people with funny socks on would line up and show them off with staff voting on the best pair. They also incorporated their wacky socks into an employee recognition program. When an employee was recognized for outstanding service, they were given a pair of fun socks to wear on Wednesdays.

Friday Funnies. Every Friday, send out an email with a few of your favorite funny TikTok, YouTube, or Instagram videos. (Since Friday is usually pretty good to begin with, you could also do it on Mondays to start the week of fun or Wednesday to keep the motivation up.)

Grateful Gifday. Choose any day of the week to set as Grateful Gifday where people share (via Slack or whatever platform is best for your team) a funny gif that represents what they're grateful for that week.

Monthly Rituals

Desk/Door Decorating Contest. Each month give a prize for the employee or department with the best decorations based on the theme of the month (could be as silly as national yo-yo month or more sincere like women's history month).

Monthly Fun Day. Web software solutions company Far Reach has a monthly Far Reach Fun Day each month where employees take time to play a board game or end the day with mini-golf or bowling.[6]

Boss for a Day. One day a month a new employee will get to be boss for the day. The week prior, they will send out an email about what the new rules are for their day as boss that's coming up like (wear hats, no emails before 10 a.m., or hot chocolate all day long).

Annual Rituals

Funny Resolutions. At the beginning of the year, have everyone give a funny resolution about something they're going to start or stop doing like "I'll stop eating all the peanut butter pretzels in the breakroom" or "I'll start unmuting myself before speaking on Zoom."

Team Service Project. Have your team choose a service project to spend one day a year giving back. It could be tied to the mission of your organization, or simply something in the community the employees care about.

Holiday Parties. Duh. Just make sure you incorporate the *Fun*damentals of Fun to make it a good time for everyone and not the holiday party or event that everyone dreads!

Other Times for Rituals

Making a ritual out of humor and fun also can be done based on your organization's schedule or important events. From a scavenger hunt during employee on-boarding to starting each quarterly sales meeting by reading something from the office humor jar, you can create rituals for almost any event. You can even create fun rituals around milestones or daily accomplishments. During the pandemic, there were hospitals that started playing "Here Comes the Sun" by The Beatles every time a Covid patient was released from the hospital to help lift the team's spirits and remind them of the successes during a time when things felt bleak.[7]

When humor and fun at work are consistent in the form of rituals and traditions, our work begins to take on more meaning to us. Sporadic doses of silliness can seem, well . . . silly in a vacuum, but when humor is strategically woven in with rituals, those silly games, odd contests, and dad jokes become part of the fabric of the culture that keeps a team thriving.

Perhaps the only thing more depressing than thinking about the fact that we spend one-third of our lives at work is that we spend another third asleep. But until I figure out how to add more humor to your sleep, you'll just have to settle for bringing more humor to work through L.A.F.T.E.R.

Humor Homework

Rituals

This week, observe the humans in your workplace like a National Geographic nature documentarian. Write down any moments of humor, levity, or fun. What types of activities elicit smiles and laughter from these work creatures? When do these behaviors occur?

Document your findings:

____

____

____

____

Reflect: How might you be able to take some of the fun things you and your colleagues already do and formalize them to create rituals?

12 Take Your Pain and Play with It

Using Humor to Boost Resilience

If you read the intro to this book, you may remember my dedicated office mate—my yellow Labrador retriever, Bridger, who loyally snores (and occasionally farts) under my desk as I write. Sadly, somewhere around Chapter 5, Bridger got cancer and didn't make to the end of this book. Not that he cared about the book—I'm 60% sure he couldn't read—but I was absolutely devastated. I've had my share of struggles and heartache in my life, but this was the saddest I think I've ever felt. He was my first dog that I raised from a puppy, he was my best friend, and we spent almost every moment of every day together. He always slept in his bed on the floor right next to my side of the bed and was my four-legged shadow from the time we woke up until it was time to get back in our beds. During his final month, I slept with him downstairs in the living room as he could no longer make it up the stairs to our bedroom.

The day we found out his cancer had spread and we had to euthanize him, several of our friends came to the vet hospital to say goodbye to him and to support Kelly and me. This was both incredible and difficult as I have a hard time being vulnerable in front of others. I was able to bury my head next to Bridger's and tell him I love him while he slowly went to sleep, and I soaked his neck in my tears. When the moment of truth came, I was not prepared. Eventually I had to really get up, say goodbye, and leave without him—and in front of other people. I could feel my breath get shorter and my body was wanting to break down and ugly cry like I hadn't done in decades. I just needed to make it home. As we got up, one of our friends said, "I'm so sorry Paul." I quickly replied, "I know, thank you. It's even worse for Kelly. Now she has to share the bed with me again." We shared a brief, sad little chuckle that was just enough to give us all a breath and get me out the door.

No, this comment wasn't the funniest thing I've ever said. In fact, it may not have even made you laugh. But, for me, that sad little chuckle was a vital hit of oxygen when I felt like I was suffocating. I don't know where that comment came from or why I said it. My brain did that on its own, and I think it was to help me in a time of distress. That one small dose of humor was just enough to help me cope with the acute stress I was feeling so I could go grieve at home with Kelly. Did making that joke relieve all my pain? Absolutely not. Was humor just a way for me to pretend the problem didn't exist? Nope. The pain was still there moments later, and is still with me today as I shed a couple tears writing this story.

As much as I'd like to think I'm special, it turns out I'm not the only person in the world whose mind has turned to humor to help them through hard times. The passing of a loyal companion isn't even close to the limit of distress that humor can buoy us through. Jake Hastings had been a firefighter, an EMT, and an Air Force medic. His nickname in the Air Force was "Dark Cloud" because he was always the one that ended up at the worst and most gruesome calls. Jake told me, "If you can imagine it, I've seen it." After his time in the Air Force, he suffered from severe post-traumatic stress disorder (PTSD) and struggled to find coping strategies that would work. He tried therapy on several occasions, but no matter how much he tried, it felt too formal, and he wasn't at a place where he could access his emotions enough to process them with a therapist. Jake's search for mental well-being eventually took a turn for the better in the unlikeliest of places—Last Best Comedy club in Bozeman, Montana. Jake began taking improv and stand-up comedy classes, and it didn't take long for him to notice that comedy unlocked something in him that had been dormant for some time: feelings. He said, ". . . the humor writing process was almost like journaling and humor gave me a way to access emotions, and also a sense of control over them." Not only is Jake now working with a therapist, but he also spends time speaking with other veterans and law enforcement professionals about the benefits of doing so. Humor alone is not therapy, and shouldn't be used as a substitute for it. However, humor does allow us to speak the untold truths about the difficulties of life. In this case, comedy was Jake's gateway drug to therapy.

A sense of humor is a built-in resiliency optimization feature in the human psyche. Chaya Ostrower's narrative study of Jewish Holocaust survivors highlights their ability to cope with the atrocities by using various types of humor. One survivor recalls, "This was the integral part of our inner, mental struggle for our human identity, the fact that we could still laugh at things. . . . I tell you this as an ex-prisoner. No matter how little it occurred, no matter how sporadic it was, or how spontaneous, it was very important. Very important!"[1] The survivors interviewed in this study were not only able to recount topics that often led to humor, but even specific stories or jokes that provided brief moments of levity. Even the smallest moment of humor can provide just enough cognitive distance to give us a brief break from our trauma because our brains can't process humor and psychological distress at the same time.[2]

There was definitely nothing funny about the Holocaust, the horrors that Jake witnessed as an Air Force medic, or Bridger dying. The point of this chapter is not to take real problems and pretend they don't exist, or for you to make light of the heavy burdens in your life. It's not about laughing *at* your problems, it's about laughing *through* them. The comment about my wife Kelly having to share the bed with me again after our dog died was an example of humor that kind of just happened. It came to me in the moment, and it was serendipitous, but it wasn't like I was intentionally trying to get through my pain with humor. That was the neurons in my brain instinctively firing on funny due to the humor habit I've created for myself over time.

Once you put your humor habit into practice, it's more likely your funny focus will kick in and provide some levity during difficult times as well—but you don't have to hope for that to happen. After all, why hope for humor when you can harness it? They say comedy equals tragedy plus time, but what they don't say is that the amount of time is up to you. (Also, I have no idea who *they* are, but they're probably the same ones who say stuff like "It is what it is" and "Everything happens for a reason.")

Throughout this book you've equipped yourself with an array of tools to combat chronic seriousness, cultivate and consume more humor, develop a funny focus, and bring humor to work. Now it's time to learn how to create your own humor from the place where the best comedy is born—the pain points in life. Think about that one hilarious comedy movie or show where a guy wakes up, he's happy, he has a wonderful marriage, his kids are well behaved, he loves his job, and his day goes great. That movie doesn't exist . . . because it would suck. The struggles, conflict, and pain are what make the characters come to life, and of course, add the elements necessary for comedy. So, let's see if we can use some timeless comedy techniques that I call "Humor Hacks" to help you mine your struggles for nuggets of humor.

The most important thing to remember when playing with these comedy tools and strategies is to not get hung up focusing on the outcome. It's the process of exercising your humor muscle and playing with funny concepts that will impact your mindset and way of being. Just like learning any new skill, the more you do it, the more natural it becomes. My friend, colleague, and stress expert Dr. Heidi Hanna describes it best. When we're learning a new skill, the neuropathways in our brain are like a dirt road. It's bumpy and slow. The more we practice and do something, eventually that road gets paved and the signals travel faster, until ultimately, it will be an information superhighway and the neurons are moving so fast that it all comes naturally. Practice your humor habit enough, and you'll teach the neurons in your brain to fire on funny.

Humor Hacks

Ask for Help

Okay, I know we discussed this in the section on bringing humor to work, but it's different when we're talking about personal struggles. Before really diving into the Humor Hacks exercises, it's important to acknowledge that this stuff isn't easy for most people. Comedians rely on one another for help working out material all the time. We'll run jokes by each other, give each other notes, and occasionally take the feedback in stride. When playing with your pain points, it's also okay to ask for help if you feel comfortable sharing with a friend. In fact, it may be a fun and different way to reach out for support or normalize what you're going through with people in your life.

My friend Amy Oestreicher did this beautifully. An actress, writer, and performer, Amy was faced with tremendous adversity due to several severe chronic medical conditions. After a total gastrectomy (removal of the stomach), Amy struggled with short bowel syndrome and had just found out she was going to need a multi-visceral transplant, which is essentially a transplant of the small intestine, liver, pancreas, and stomach (if she had one), all at the same time. Understandably, Amy was quite nervous for this procedure, and she reached out to me and a few other friends. She just came right out and asked us to come up with something funny about transplants or her situation to make her laugh the week before her procedure. I found a photo of her, created a meme out of it (Figure 12.1), and sent it her way.

Amy loved it and said it made her day! She even shared it with some friends who were going through similar medical complications as hers. Sadly, about two years later, Amy passed away. She was a model of resilience, extremely creative, and was an expert at playing with her pain through art, music, and theater so she was well equipped with the tools to help herself with humor. You might be too. But some days are tougher than others, and sometimes you may

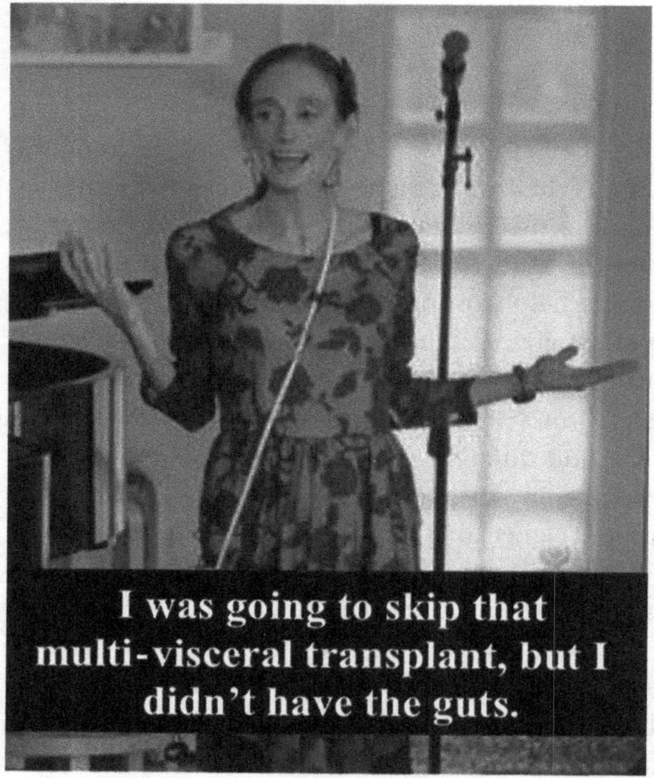

I was going to skip that multi-visceral transplant, but I didn't have the guts.

FIGURE 12.1 Amy O meme. (Credit: Marilyn Oestreicher)

not have the energy to cheer yourself up. You can always do what Amy did and ask for a little humor help with your own situation to find the humor *in it*, help you get *through it*, or distract you *from it*.

Exaggeration

Exaggeration is used in all forms of comedy, including writing, improv, stand-up, movies, and TV. The idea is simple. You continue to heighten or exaggerate a concept until it becomes ridiculous or funny. The key to exaggeration is that it needs to be wildly exaggerated to become funny, not just exaggerated a bit. Humorist Dave Barry is an expert with this technique. Here's an example where he talks about how men worry about messing up the laundry:

> "We worry that if we get just one variable wrong, we will find ourselves facing a wrathful spouse, who is holding up *a garment that was once a valued brassiere of normal dimensions, but is now suitable only as a sun hat for a small, two-headed squirrel.*"[3] A sun hat for a small two-headed squirrel? Ridiculous.

Exaggeration, like all the humor hacks you'll learn in this chapter, can be used to find humor in the stressful, annoying, or painful parts of life. Let's take a fairly common and mildly stressful situation like your car breaking down, for instance. You're on the side of the road waiting for a tow truck and you text home to your partner, "Hey, the car broke down and I've been waiting for a tow for an hour. I'll be home as soon as I can." At this point, your stress is building, and the situation is getting more frustrating. Why not heighten it with a little exaggeration and send another text? "Please tell the kids I love them, wish them luck in college, and text me photos when they produce grandchildren." Heightening the situation to a ridiculous extreme immediately provides perspective. Yes, the situation is annoying, but when it's catastrophized in such a ludicrous way, it frames the situation with the appropriate amount of relative importance. It also keeps the stress, anger, or frustration from climbing, and perhaps, even deescalates you from an 8 out of 10 to a 5 or 6. Not to mention, the person on the receiving end of the text may also benefit from the perspective and humorous intervention as well as knowing that you're not freaking out.

An easy way to practice with exaggeration is with the formula along the lines of "I was so ________________ that ________________." You can use any difficult situation or pain point you've experienced. For example, if you've had a string of unfortunate car accidents, then how bad are things going to get?

"I've made so many claims, my insurance company now only covers me for a donkey-powered rickshaw." Another tip: try to find the funniest words too. At first I thought of *horse-drawn wagon*, but *donkey* is funnier than *horse* and *rickshaw* is funnier than *wagon*.

Try it with some of these or use your own formula:

I'm so tired that ________________________________.

My attention span is so short ________________________.

I've stared at a computer screen so long ________________.

Try your own! ________________________________.

As you apply the humor hacks in this section, you'll notice that you can combine the tools and use humor hacks together. Exaggeration is one that can be used with almost any other comedic device—including the humor habits in the previous chapters. You can also use the concept of exaggeration to play with your pain without ever putting it on paper or into words. For instance, Casey Shank, a small business owner and therapist, started losing her hair a few years ago after undergoing chemotherapy for ovarian cancer. She showed up to one of her chemo appointments wearing a funky head wrap. The oncology nurses loved it and thought it was fun, so to the delight of the oncology team, she heightened it and made her head wraps funkier and more fun each time (Figure 12.2)!

Casey used exaggeration as well as the concept of thinking "fun over funny" (Chapter 8). She had fun with her head wraps and then made them bigger, better, and in some cases, brighter for each appointment!

FIGURE 12.2 Casey's head wraps. (Credit: Casey Shank)

The Comic Triple

The comic triple is a go-to technique used by people who write comedy, who perform comedy, and who can count to three. You simply make a list of three things about your topic with the first two being obvious or serious, and the third being something funny, surprising, or different. For example, I use the comic triple in the final sentence of my bio for speaking engagements: "Paul's work has been highlighted in the *New York Times*, *Forbes*, and on his mom's refrigerator." Similarly, when people ask about what I do, I'll tell people, "I help you create a positive work culture, and get your employees engaged . . . but I won't plan their weddings." We're starting a pattern with the first two items and breaking the pattern with the third one. One of the best ways to generate humor is with the element of surprise or incongruity, and the comic triple gives us a nice plug and play formula to utilize it. The unexpected incongruity of the third thing is the spark that lights the funny fire.

Before we play with the comic triple formula with one of your pain points or struggles, let's do it with something more neutral like a bio about yourself or what you do.

Hi, my name is ________________ and
I ______________, I ______________, and I ______________.
(obvious/serious) (obvious/serious) (funny/surprising/different)

This doesn't have to be hilarious to start. Just make it fit the formula. For example, my name is Paul and I'm a speaker, an author, and cheeseburger connoisseur. The third thing can be anything different or fun about you like a hobby, talent, or fun fact. This is something you can play with during small talk, introductions, or for your LinkedIn bio.

About a year after facilitating a workshop with one of the disaster recovery and business continuity groups I spoke to, one participant followed up with me. He told me that explaining what he did for a living used to be a pain point for him because people either didn't understand or they just tuned out. He was excited to report that the comic triple formula helped because it made his formerly awkward answer to the "What do you do?" question more succinct, but also funnier and more intriguing. He shared that now when people ask what his job entails, he says, "I think of all the potential disasters that could happen to our company, then I create a plan to address them . . . I guess you could say I'm a professional buzzkill." He said it always gets a laugh and sparks more conversation!

Okay, now that you've warmed up with a neutral version of the comic triple, it's time to play with a pain point. Think of a pain point about being you. It could be something permanent or temporary. While you can do this exercise with deeper, more significant pains like getting fired from a job or getting a divorce, I suggest starting with something with a little less gravity. You can go back to the humor homework in Chapter 6 and use one of the things you listed there or come up with something new. Some examples may include:

- Being short, tall, big, small, and so on.
- Not having a car.
- Having a broken leg.
- Being a single parent.
- Having a chronic ailment like migraines, arthritis, anxiety, or ADHD.
- Being in an underrepresented group at your work (the only woman, person of color, oldest, youngest, etc.).
- Having bad vision or another impairment or disability.

Once you've selected your pain point that you'd like to "play" with, it's time to put it through the following formula to reframe it with humor and create your comic triple.

1. Flip it
2. Triple it
3. Deliver it

Flip it:

You're going to flip the narrative of this pain point as if it were actually a positive or a superpower. Try to list as many positives about this pain point. Some of them could be legitimately positive, while others might be sarcastic or even ridiculous.

Flip it example:

Pain point—Being short.
Positive things about being short (feel free to make your list longer, mine is . . . well, short).

- I don't hit my head on things.
- Lots of leg room on flights and long drives.
- Short people live longer.
- Every bed is big enough.
- Less likely to get struck by lightning than tall people.
- Nobody asks for my help putting their carry-on in the overhead bin.

Triple it:

Pick three of the positive items you brainstormed to put into the comic triple formula, making sure the first two are the most obvious, normal, or serious, and the last one is the most absurd or different. If the last one isn't absurd or different yet, then in the next step you may have to heighten or exaggerate it!

Triple It Example

1. Obvious/serious: Short guys live longer.
2. Obvious/serious: They don't need big beds.
3. Funny/Surprising/Different: They have a tons of leg room in the car.

As you can see, my third one needs some work. It's not that funny or different. I'll work on it in the next step.

Deliver it:

This is where you punch it up and add some context like a set up or introduction and/or add some flare to the third one to make it stand out from the other two.

Deliver It Example

"I used to think no girl would ever date me because I was short, but it turns out there are advantages to dating a short guy. As

> a short guy, I'll live longer, I take up less room in bed, and I'll always let you drive because I have to stay in my car seat."

As you can see, I added some context and got a little more specific about my pain point. It wasn't just about being short, it was specifically that dating was hard as a short guy. That helped me frame my three positives better, so instead of my initial thought that "short guys don't need big beds," it was that I would take up less room in bed with a partner. Finally, I was able to use the humor hack of exaggeration to make my third part of the comic triple (the leg room in the car) funnier. At first, I thought about my feet not reaching the pedals, then not even reaching the floor, but I kept heightening it, so you end with a visual that I'm so small, I'm buckled up in a car seat like a toddler.

Here's another quick one without all the explanation. The pain point is that I mostly work by myself from home:

> "There are advantages to working from home. I have a flexible schedule, no commute, and when my co-workers annoy me, I just lock them in a crate for an hour."

Okay, now you try it!
Pain point: ____________________

Flip it:

Triple it:

1. Obvious or serious ____________________
2. Obvious or serious ____________________
3. Funny/surprising/different ____________________

Deliver it:

Nice work! Give yourself a high five, a pat on the back, or a small vacation home in the south of France.

You don't necessarily have to do the "flip it" step with your pain point either if you don't want to. Maybe you can't or don't want to think of any positives—even if they are ridiculous. Perhaps you're describing how you're really feeling or telling someone about what you're dealing with and don't want to sugar coat it.

I explained the comic triple when doing some work with Sun Pharmaceuticals on behalf of the Association for Applied and Therapeutic Humor (AATH). Specifically, we were working with people living with psoriasis, providing humor tools explaining the therapeutic benefits of humor, and how to apply humor when living with a chronic condition. Some of the examples generated using the comic triple with this group included:

- Explaining what psoriasis is to someone for the first time: "Psoriasis is an autoimmune condition that causes a buildup of skin cells, scaling, and an abnormal amount of conversations about lotion."
- Explaining your symptoms to a friend, co-worker, or a doctor/nurse: "My most common psoriasis symptoms are that it makes my skin flake, makes me itch, and makes me break out in long sleeves."
- When the doctor asks you how you've been treating your psoriasis: "I treat my psoriasis with medication, light therapy, and a vacuum."

By using humor to play with our pain, we're reclaiming control of our own story and boosting our resilience. We're all battling something in our lives that others may know nothing about. There are certainly people with personal struggles or chronic conditions who aren't ready or comfortable using humor to cope with their situation. But for those who are, the ability to use humor as a tool to connect, normalize, cope with, or simply explain what they're going through can be an incredibly effective well-being strategy to thrive in or outside of work.

Keep creating as many comic triples as you can for neutral topics in emails or texts to friends to practice, and then continue to play with pain points using the tried-and-true comedic formula. Now, when you go back and read this book again someday (why not, right?) you'll notice how often I used the comic triple to break things up and try to give a laugh.

Comparison

This one is simple. You compare your situation or feelings to something else. One of the easiest ways to get started with comparison is the use of similes or metaphors. From what I remember from elementary school, a metaphor is a figure of speech where one thing symbolizes another and a simile is pretty much the same thing, but you use the words *like* or *as* when you compare them. (By the way, this always confused me. Why do there need to be two terms for this? Why can't we just call all these metaphors? I mean, "Life is a highway" is a metaphor, but "Life is *like* a highway" is a simile. "A metaphor is a sad Instagram post . . . no likes" is a metaphor but "A metaphor is *like* a sad Instagram post . . . no likes" is a simile. This is probably the longest and most confusing of my parenthetical asides, I hope you enjoyed the peek inside my brain.) Fortunately, it doesn't matter if what you write is actually a metaphor or a simile, or simaphor—you don't have to turn this in and you're not being graded on it. Let's look at a few!

- The construction outside my office is a symphony of displeasure.
- Coordinating everyone's schedules is like solving a Rubik's cube with my tongue.

- I've got a migraine. My head feels like a boob mid-mammogram.
- Having shingles is like wearing fiberglass Spanx.
- That email is as long as a CVS receipt.

Okay, you get the idea. Now it's time for you to try! As you play with these, try swapping out different words and don't forget to exaggerate. My mind first thought of doing a Rubik's cube with my feet, but doing it with my tongue is more extreme. At first, I thought of a *fiberglass sweater*, but *Spanx* is a much funnier word and image . . . and of course, *boob* is always a funny word.

Create your own metaphor from misery or simile from suffering!

Pain point: ______________________________

Metaphor or simile comparison: ______________________________

____

Another way to compare your point or feeling to something else is simply by making a list of all the things you can think of associated with your situation and another list of all the things that come to mind with the comparison. The more farfetched or different they seem, the more likely you are to find some funny comparisons. Here's an example that I started during the pandemic, and although I never really struck humor gold out of it, it's a good example of the mining process.

Pain Point: Living in a pandemic	**Comparison: The Little Mermaid**
Stuck at home	Lives Under the Sea
Virtual meetings	Wants to be where the people are
Washing hands longer and more often	Collects treasures from humans
Social distancing	Best friend Sebastian the Crab
People hoarding toilet paper and sanitizer	Ursula the witch

What do you notice that could be compared? Of course, being stuck at home in the pandemic goes along with wanting to be where the people are. Collecting treasures from the human world goes along with all those lovely people who were stashing toilet paper and sanitizer. The Little Mermaid was a hoarder! Remember when she just took a fork? I feel like in the next movie she's going to open a pawn shop—or more like a prawn shop (see, I told you there was nothing comedically great here, but you can see how one thing leads to another). It also seems like there could be something with living under the sea. Perhaps it would go with being a mermaid and washing our hands so often. Looking back at this list now, the best I could come up with is "Living in the pandemic, I felt like The Little Mermaid. I was just trying to keep my head above water, I wanted to be where the people were, and the only person I got to hang out with was a crab all the time." Meh, it doesn't make me crack up either, but remember, this isn't for a grade, so if you don't like yours, just try another one with a different comparison. It's all about the process.

Here's another comparison example regarding me not having children:

> "It's probably best that I don't have kids. For me, a kid would be like a boat. At first, I'd be stoked to come up with a cool name for it, then I'd be like . . . I don't know how to take care of this thing. I hate that it's always wet. Maybe I should sell it."

Now you try it! Make a list of all the things associated with your pain point, and then a list of things associated with something to compare it to. You can change out the comparison as many times as you want until you come up with something you like.

My pain point:

Comparison:

Potential funny pairings or observations:

Mash-Ups

Here, you'll select two things about yourself and see if you can create a little comedy mash-up. You can choose two pain points, like being broke and overweight, or you can choose just one pain point and any other characteristic or trait about yourself like being broke and loving to cook. Here are a couple of examples from my life and pain points:

> "I'm bald and I'm white. Which apparently is soooo cool if you're an eagle. They're super popular. I'm only popular with sunscreen manufacturers and dermatologists."
>
> "I'm nearly deaf in one ear, and I work at home alone. Do you know how annoying it is to be talking to yourself and then yell out 'Whaaaaaat!?'"

It's your turn! Once you have your two topics, layer the comparison humor hack on top and make a list of attributes that come to mind about each. Is there anything that sticks out right away? Are there any obvious similarities? Once you have your lists, begin using other humor hacks like exaggeration and comic triples, and try using similes to see if you can create some magic. Remember, it may feel like a bumpy dirt road at first, but the more you do it the sooner you'll have that funny freeway running through your brain.

First pain point: ____________________
Second pain point or trait: ____________________
Funny observations or comparisons: ____________________
____
____
____

Puns and Wordplay

"I went to a children's theater and instead of a stage, they performed on palettes of dictionaries. It was a play on words."

I wanted to begin this section with a pun about a play on words, and that's what I came up with. I don't have kids, but sometimes when I tell jokes, I identify as a dad. If you like puns and wordplay, it can be a fun and pretty easy way to create humor. The simple key to a pun is that there must be at least one word that has a similar sound, meaning, or spelling as another word. Sometimes the words will sound the same or very similar, but they're spelled different:

"Don't make puns about German sausage—they're the wurst."

Other puns will use words that are spelled exactly the same, but have different meanings like this:

"Never make puns about menstruation . . . period."

Keep in mind with the puns that sound the same (worst and wurst), you can also use words that rhyme as well. For example:

"When do you eat German sausage as an appetizer instead of a main course? When it's brought first."

Brought sounds like *brat*, but *first*" simply rhymes with *wurst*. (This pun is even better with a German accent because "brought first" sounds even more like bratwurst.)

Now it's time to learn how to make some puns. One way is to start with the end in mind. For example, I knew I wanted to begin this section with a pun about "a play on words." From there, I knew I would need to find double meanings, sounds, or rhymes with at least one of those words. You can make a list if you want or just do it in your head. My mind automatically went to the thought of kids playing on a playground for the word *play*. But how would they play on words? I thought about kids playing literally on huge letters that they could climb on, but none of that seemed pun-worthy. Then, I thought of another meaning for the word *play*: a theater performance on top of a bunch of words is a "play" on words.

Beginning with the end in mind is one way to do it, but if you're trying to make puns out of the pain points in your life, it's probably going to come to you based on the words associated with your situation. Let's say you had a difficult time locating the area of the hospital you were supposed to go to, which made you late to your chemotherapy appointment. Think of words applicable to the situation like hospital, parking, late, chemotherapy, treatment, and so on. Then, look for double meanings or trying to rhyme with different words. Take *chemo*, for example: *bemo*, *demo*, *gemo*, *femo*, *Nemo*! *Finding Nemo . . . finding chemo*.

> "Sorry I'm late. Pixar should make a movie about me trying to get here today . . . Finding Chemo!"

Or, think of a word that's common to your condition and what other meanings there are for that word. Here's an example:

> "I sprained my ankle again! My doctor should prescribe me medical marijuana since I'm so good at rolling joints."

First off, this statement is true about my ankle. It rolls faster than a teenage girl's eyes at a dad joke. The steps to this pun were:

Think of associated words: ankle, sprain, joint, limp, swollen, and so on. I saw the word *joint* and knew there had to be something there with the double meaning of that word. (For those of you innocent folks who don't know what a joint is . . . it's the place where two bones connect.) To my nerdy delight, the term *rolling a joint* came to my mind and I realized *rolling* could also be used for my ankle . . . a double double-entendre!

Here's another one with two plays on words that I created after a doctor's appointment:

> "After 60 years running, you'd think the Journal of Cardiology would have a higher circulation."

Running and circulation both have double meanings making them pun-worthy. What about your pain points? Can you make some puns with the struggles you've got going on? Let's give it a shot.

Pain point: ____

Words associated with my pain point or situation: ____________

____

____

Preceding words with double meanings, or other words that sound like them: ____

____

____

Play around with some ideas: ____________________________

____

____

____

My Pain Point Pun: ______________________________________

____

____

Make the Laughs Last

This one isn't a full hack on its own, but may help you sharpen some of the humor you're creating—particularly if you share any of the humor with others. Essentially, once you create a joke, pun, meme, or have a funny story, when possible, arrange the words so that the funniest part is at the end. Or if I were doing that with the previous sentence, I would have said "arrange the words so the end is the funniest part." For example, when I was speaking to a group of doctors, I told them that I was married to a veterinarian. I said, "I think being married to an animal doctor is probably similar to being married to an MD, the only difference being, when I get sick . . . how she takes my temperature." When I first thought of that joke it came to me as ". . . the only difference being how she takes my temperature when I get sick." The humorous part of the statement is about how she takes my temperature. Once that part is said, people begin to laugh. Once I continue speaking to say, "when I get sick," people will quiet down again to hear the rest of what I have to say, thus halting their laughter. Comedians call this "stepping on the laugh." The best-case scenario for a punchline is that the last words you say are the funniest part and you can pause and let them fully laugh.

You can look back at the last section on puns and imagine if they were written with the pun in a different place. "The wurst puns are puns about German sausage" just doesn't work as well as "Puns about German sausage are the wurst." In Chapter 7, I mentioned getting help from AI and finding the Chat GPT joke: "Why did the math book ask for help? Because it had too many problems and couldn't solve them all on its own" Not bad for a computer, really. But I reworded it to "Having a lot of problems you can't solve on your own, just means you're human . . . or a math book." This is something you can use to punch up your punchlines whether you're creating them just for your own well-being, telling jokes to your friends, or adding some humor to your next presentation.

Unfortunately/Fortunately

This is an improv game or warm-up activity that is very easy to play on your own, even silently in your head throughout the day. You just think of the pain point, pet peeve, or struggle you're going through and say "Unfortunately ________________" and then follow it up with a positive reframe "Fortunately ____________." The fun thing about this is that the "fortunately" part doesn't need to be serious, and in fact, the more ridiculous the better. It's also important to remember that this game is for you to play with your own pain, as throwing a "fortunately" or "at least" out at someone regarding their struggles is never helpful. Here are a few examples to get you started:

> "Unfortunately, I'll need to work through the weekend. Fortunately, that's less depressing than watching my football team lose again!"
>
> "Unfortunately, I didn't get the promotion. Fortunately, I don't have to organize my files for my replacement!"
>
> "Unfortunately, I have to prep for this colonoscopy. Fortunately, I'm going to lose a few pounds!"

Using this format might even lead you to playing with the content more and creating your own joke out of it: "I wanted to lose weight before my wedding, so I scheduled a colonoscopy." Or using the comic triple: "You should really get a colonoscopy so you can detect cancer early, live longer, and fit in your tux." Unfortunately, this is the last humor hack of the chapter. Fortunately, you can complete them as many times as you want. Your turn:

Unfortunately, ________________________________.

Fortunately, ________________________________.

Unfortunately, ________________________________.

Fortunately, ________________________________.

If "Unfortunately/Fortunately" gets too clunky in your head, you can always use "at least." If you intentionally play this game in your head enough, your brain will start jumping to your "fortunatelys" without you even thinking about it. I've played this game mentally for so long that I believe this is where the initial thought came from when I joked about Kelly having to sleep in the same bed as me after Bridger died. At some point my mind said, "At least you'll get to sleep upstairs again," and while that specific thought provided no solace in a moment of intense pain, it did lead to the brief funny comment that was the intervention I needed.

Have fun playing with all of these humor hacks by starting with some everyday pet peeves or annoyances, and slowly working your way up to playing with the pain of more difficult struggles. You don't have to show any of your comedic brilliance to anyone if you don't want to (besides, would they really get it anyway?) or you can show off your comedic chops, and perhaps, inspire others to find humor in their own struggles.

Conclusion

I received a lot of advice and feedback while writing this book. Some people advised me to make it either a book strictly about humor at work or a personal development book, but not both. Others thought I shouldn't include such heavy topics like cancer or my dog dying. But that's not how our brains, our emotions, or our lives work. Our personal struggles affect us on the job, and unless you work in Vegas, what happens at work doesn't stay there either. That's the whole point. Life is hard and messy, but it's also wonderful and fun and funny. Those things are often intertwined, and to write a book about finding the humor in life, you have to include all aspects of life—even the shitty ones.

Once you establish your humor habit, you'll not only be able to take life's lemons and make your lemonade a little sweeter, but perhaps even open your own lemonade stand and share it with others. I love the feeling of making people laugh, but I wasn't always aware of the immense power of humor. You can harness that power to not only refuel yourself, but to bring people together, brighten someone's day, or spark a brief moment of joy providing temporary relief to someone in pain.

One thing about comedians that people don't talk about is how environmentally conscious they are. They recycle all their material. There's a reason stand-up comics go on tour—because you can't do the same hour-long set at the same comedy club to the same crowd every weekend. They go spread those same jokes all over the world to new audiences. Don't be afraid to recycle your humor to make new people laugh.

I remember a dinner with my family when I was in high school. The waiter asked us how the food was, and my stepdad, Dave, replied, "It's great, you're a good cook!" The waiter laughed and said, "If only!" That was probably the nineteenth time I heard Dave say that to a waiter or waitress and I rolled my eyes in embarrassment. I've heard it hundreds of times since then, but it hits different now. What I didn't realize then was that the joke wasn't for himself, for me, or for the rest of our family. It was for the waiter. It was simply to share a moment, break the ice, and put a tiny drop of sweetener out there in case they were feeling like they had been sucking lemons all day. Dave wasn't looking to *get* a laugh, he was looking to *give* a laugh.

To this day, I recycle my stepdad's line as well as plenty of my own jokes in daily interactions with strangers and friends. (Kelly knows exactly where I'm going every time I grab a miniature bottle of water or half sized can of soda—"Now I know what a normal sized man feels like when he holds a bottle of water!") It's easy to get caught up in our own lives or to compare our insides with other people's outsides and assume we're the only ones struggling. Don't be afraid to be generous with your humor and give laughs daily. Shared laughter is empathy in action, and the world needs more empathy.

This is it! That feeling you get when you're on the final page of your book. Your mind starts wandering thinking about what it all means, what you'll read next, and how bad you have to pee (just one more minute, I swear). I hope the concepts in this book help you start experiencing more humor in your life, not by chance, but by choice. Apply the strategies in this book as many times as you want until they become easier and more natural to you. Remember, humor is not a talent. Humor is a habit. Now that the book has been read, your movie begins. Don't live your life as an actor in a drama. You're the director, and it can be a comedy. And . . . action!

P.S. I'd love to see the humor you created from the humor hacks, hear how you implemented the principles of L.A.F.T.E.R. at work, or how the humor habits are working for you! Share your takeaways from the book on social media and tag me @paulosincup and hashtag #TheHumorHabit.

Endnotes

Introduction

1. Anderer, J. (2023, August 29). Funny file not found: Artificial intelligence tells jokes, but still doesn't get humor. Study Finds. https://studyfinds.org/ai-jokes-still-doesnt-get-humor/
2. Eichenseher, T. (2023, February 7). Success and happiness: Which is most important? Psych Central. https://psychcentral.com/blog/does-success-lead-to-happiness#success-and-happiness
3. Ford, Thomas E., Lappi, S.K., & Holden, C.J. (2016). Personality, humor styles and happiness: Happy people have positive humor styles. *Europe's Journal of Psychology*, 12(3), 320–337. https://doi.org/10.5964/ejop.v12i3.1160

Chapter 1

1. Aaker, J.L., & Bagdonas, N. (2021). *Humor, seriously: Why humor is a secret weapon in business and life and how anyone can harness it. Even you.* Currency.
2. Azagba, S., & Sharaf, M.F. (2011). Psychosocial working conditions and the utilization of health care services. *BMC Public Health*, *11*, 642. https://doi.org/10.1186/1471-2458-11-642
3. American Psychological Association. (n.d.). Stress in America. American Psychological Association. Retrieved January 27, 2022, from https://www.apa.org/news/press/releases/stress/2014/stress-report.pdf
4. Seppälä, E., & Cameron, K. (2017, May 8). Proof that positive work cultures are more productive. *Harvard Business Review*. Retrieved January 27, 2022, from https://hbr.org/2015/12/proof-that-positive-work-cultures-are-

more-productive?utm_medium=social&utm_campaign=hbr&utm_source=facebook&tpcc=orgsocial_edit&fbclid=IwAR3kRk-XnHDZeGPu2qQiT5ocxPzUkjibUSmE0tRxbh3YaKUbLWxhHOrOsAE

5. Westerlund, H., Nyberg, A., Bernin, P., Hyde, M., Oxenstierna, G., Jäppinen, P., Väänänen, A., & Theorell, T. (2010). Managerial leadership is associated with employee stress, health, and sickness absence independently of the demand-control-support model. *Work* (Reading, Mass.), *37*(1), 71–79. https://doi.org/10.3233/WOR-2010-1058
6. Workplace stress. The American Institute of Stress. (2021, February 9). Retrieved January 27, 2022, from https://www.stress.org/workplace-stress
7. Mcfeeeley, S., & Wigert, B. (2021, December 7). This fixable problem costs U.S. businesses $1 trillion. Gallup.com. Retrieved January 27, 2022, from https://www.gallup.com/workplace/247391/fixable-problem-costs-businesses-trillion.aspx
8. Gallup State of the Global Workplace Report. Gallup.com. https://www.gallup.com/workplace/349484/state-of-the-global-workplace.aspx
9. American Psychological Association. (2020, October 20). Stress in America 2020 survey signals a growing national mental health crisis [Press release]. http://www.apa.org/news/press/releases/2020/10/stress-mental-health-crisis
10. Seppala, E., Emma Schootstra, D.D., & Claman, P. (2018, March 20). Research: For better brainstorming, tell an embarrassing story. *Harvard Business Review*. Retrieved April 6, 2022, from https://hbr.org/2017/10/research-for-better-brainstorming-tell-an-embarrassing-story
11. Ware, B. (2019). *The top five regrets of the dying: A life transformed by the dearly departing*. Hay House Australia.
12. Guardian News and Media. (2012, February 1). Top five regrets of the dying. *The Guardian*. Retrieved April 7, 2022, from https://www.theguardian.com/lifeandstyle/2012/feb/01/top-five-regrets-of-the-dying

Chapter 2

1. Steinhilber, B. (2018, July 26). How comedians Jeannie and Jim Gaffigan used humor to cope with a brain tumor. NBCNews.com. Retrieved January 18, 2022, from https://www.nbcnews.com/better/pop-culture/how-comedians-jeannie-jim-gaffigan-used-humor-cope-tragedy-ncna894581

2. Roman, L., & Cousins, N. (1982). *Anatomy of an illness*. Hamner/Gershwin Productions.
3. Bains G., Berk L., Lohman E., Daher N., & Miranda B. (2017). Decrease in inflammation (CRP) and heart rate through mirthful laughter. *FASEB Journal*, *31*(1)(suppl), 697.7.
4. *Merriam-Webster*. (n.d.). Humor definition & meaning. Merriam-Webster.com. Retrieved January 19, 2022, from https://www.merriam-webster.com/dictionary/humor.
5. *Merriam-Webster*. (n.d.). *Laughing* definition and meaning. Merriam-Webster.com. Retrieved January 19, 2022, from https://www.merriam-webster.com/dictionary/laughing.
6. Yim, J.E. (2016). Therapeutic benefits of laughter in mental health: A theoretical review. *The Tohoku Journal of Experimental Medicine*, *239*(3), 243–249. https://doi.org/10.1620/tjem.239.243.
7. Nasr, S. (2013). No laughing matter: Laughter is good psychiatric medicine: Laughter can be helpful for treating mood disorders and other conditions. *Current Psychiatry*, *12*, 20.
8. Jerabek, I. (2023, August 30). Can you laugh your stress away?—New study examines the cathartic benefits of humor. Cision PRWeb provides efficient communication tools to continuously engage with target audiences across multiple online channels. https://www.prweb.com/releases/can-you-laugh-your-stress-away---new-study-examines-looks-at-the-cathartic-benefits-of-humor-301912851.html
9. Bains, G.S., Berk, L.S., Daher, N., Lohman, E., Schwab, E., Petrofsky, J., & Deshpande, P. (2014). The effect of humor on short-term memory in older adults: A new component for whole-person wellness. *Advances in Mind-Body Medicine*, 28(2), 16–24.
10. Ghayas, S., & Malik, F. (2013, December 31). Sense of humor as predictor of creativity level in university undergraduates. *Journal of Behavioural Sciences*, 23(2): 49–61.
11. Lewis, T. (2005). Creativity a framework for the design/problem solving discourse in technology education. *Journal of Technology Education*, *17*(1). https://doi.org/10.21061/jte.v17i1.a.3
12. Abel, M. (2002). Humor, stress, and coping strategies, *Humor*, *15*(4), 365–381. https://doi.org/10.1515/humr.15.4.365.
13. Ford, T.E., Ferguson, M.A., Brooks, J.L., & Hagadone, K.M. (2004). Coping sense of humor reduces effects of stereotype threat on women's

math performance. *Personality and Social Psychology Bulletin*, *30*(5), 643–653. https://doi.org/10.1177/0146167203262851

14. Tagalidou, N., Loderer, V., Distlberger, E., & Laireiter, A.-R. (2018). Feasibility of a humor training to promote humor and decrease stress in a subclinical sample: A single-arm pilot study. *Frontiers in Psychology*, *9*. https://doi.org/10.3389/fpsyg.2018.00577
15. Berk, L.S., Felten, D.L., Tan, S.A., Bittman, B.B., & Westengard, J. (2001). Modulation of neuroimmune parameters during the eustress of humor-associated mirthful laughter. *Alternative Therapies in Health and Medicine*, 7(2), 62–72, 74–76.
16. Berk, L.S., Tan, S.A., Fry, W.F., et al. (1989). Neuroendocrine and stress hormone changes during mirthful laughter. *American Journal of the Medical Sciences*, *298*(6), 390–396.
17. Bennett, M.P., & Lengacher, C. (2009). Humor and laughter may influence health IV. Humor and immune function. *Evidence-Based Complementary and Alternative Medicine*, *6*(2):159–164.
18. Sakurada, K., Konta, T., Watanabe, M., Ishizawa, K., Ueno, Y., Yamashita, H., & Kayama, T. (2020). Associations of frequency of laughter with risk of all-cause mortality and cardiovascular disease incidence in a general population: Findings from the Yamagata Study. *Journal of Epidemiology*, *30*(4), 188–193. https://doi.org/10.2188/jea.JE20180249
19. Tan, S.A., Tan, L.G., Lukman, S.T., & Berk, L.S. (2007). Humor, as an adjunct therapy in cardiac rehabilitation, attenuates catecholamines and myocardial infarction recurrence. *Advances in Mind-Body Medicine*, 22(3–4), 8–12.
20. Skerrett, P.J. (2010, November 25). Laugh and be thankful—It's good for the heart. *Harvard Health*. Retrieved January 24, 2022, from https://www.health.harvard.edu/blog/laugh-and-be-thankful-its-good-for-the-heart-20101124839
21. Tse, M.M., Lo, A.P., Cheng, T.L., Chan, E.K., Chan, A.H., & Chung, H.S. (2010). Humor therapy: Relieving chronic pain and enhancing happiness for older adults. *Journal of Aging Research*, 343574. https://doi.org/10.4061/2010/343574
22. Strean, W.B. (2009). Laughter prescription. *Canadian Family Physician (Medecin de Famille Canadien)*, *55*(10), 965–967.
23. Bennett, P.N., Parsons, T., Ben-Moshe, R., Weinberg, M., Neal, M., Gilbert, K., Rawson, H., Ockerby, C., Finlay, P., & Hutchinson, A. (2014). Laughter

and humor therapy in dialysis. *Seminars in Dialysis*, 27(5), 488–493. https://doi.org/10.1111/sdi.12194

24. Pérez-Aranda, A., Hofmann, J., Feliu-Soler, A., Ramírez-Maestre, C., Andrés-Rodríguez, L., Ruch, W., & Luciano, J.V. (2019). Laughing away the pain: A narrative review of humour, sense of humour and pain. *European Journal of Pain* (London, England), 23(2), 220–233. https://doi.org/10.1002/ejp.1309
25. Mesmer-Magnus, J., Glew, D., & Viswesvaran (Vish), C. (2012). A meta-analysis of positive humor in the workplace. *Journal of Managerial Psychology*, 27, 155–190. 10.1108/02683941211199554
26. Kurtz, L.E., & Algoe, S.B. (2016). When sharing a laugh means sharing more: Testing the role of shared laughter on short-term interpersonal consequences. *Journal of Nonverbal Behavior*, *41*(1), 45–65. https://doi.org/10.1007/s10919-016-0245-9
27. Manninen, S., Tuominen, L., Dunbar, R.I., Karjalainen, T., Hirvonen, J., Arponen, E., Hari, R., Jääskeläinen, I.P., Sams, M., & Nummenmaa, L. (2017). Social laughter triggers endogenous opioid release in humans. *The Journal of Neuroscience*, 37(25), 6125–6131. https://doi.org/10.1523/jneurosci.0688-16.2017
28. Gonot-Schoupinsky, F., & Garip, G., (2019). Prescribing laughter to increase well-being in healthy adults: An exploratory mixed methods feasibility study of the Laughie. *European Journal of Integrative Medicine*, 56–64. doi:10.1016/j.eujim.2019.01.005
29. Schiffman, R. (2020, October 1). Laughter may be effective medicine for these trying times. *New York Times*. Retrieved January 24, 2022, from https://www.nytimes.com/2020/10/01/well/mind/laughter-may-be-effective-medicine-for-these-trying-times.html
30. BBC. (2022, January 1). Prescribed Bristol comedy course could help trauma recovery. BBC News. Retrieved January 24, 2022, from https://www.bbc.com/news/uk-england-bristol-59758335
31. Drinko, C. (n.d.). The improv anxiety treatment? *Psychology Today*. Retrieved January 24, 2022, from https://www.psychologytoday.com/us/blog/play-your-way-sane/201912/the-improv-anxiety-treatment
32. Chillag, A. (2018, August 20). How an improv class is helping the anxious. CNN. Retrieved January 24, 2022, from https://www.cnn.com/2018/07/05/health/improv-for-anxiety-staying-well/index.html

33. Lipman, F. (2019, March 31). The healing power of laughter. Retrieved January 31, 2022, from https://drfranklipman.com/2019/03/05/the-healing-power-of-laughter/

Chapter 3

1. Phillips, K.A., Ospina, N.S., Rodriguez-Gutierrez, R., et al. (2018). Humor during clinical practice: Analysis of recorded clinical encounters. *Journal of the American Board of Family Medicine*, *31*(2), 270–278.
2. Singh Ospina, N., Phillips, K.A., Rodriguez-Gutierrez, R., et al. (2019). Eliciting the patient's agenda—secondary analysis of recorded clinical encounters. *Journal of General Internal Medicine*, *34*(1), 36–40.
3. Alexander Fleming. (2023, May 22). Science History Institute. https://sciencehistory.org/education/scientific-biographies/alexander-fleming/#:~:text=Somehow%2C%20in%20preparing%20the%20culture,various%20molds%20were%20being%20cultured
4. The accidental invention of Play-Doh. (2019, November 12). *Smithsonian Magazine*, Smithsonian.com. https://www.smithsonianmag.com/innovation/accidental-invention-play-doh-180973527/
5. About Us. Post. Accessed August 23, 2023, from https://www.post-it.com/3M/en_US/post-it/contact-us/about-us/
6. Stuart, H. (2015, June 8). 8 companies that celebrate mistakes. Happy Ltd. https://www.happy.co.uk/blogs/8-companies-that-celebrate-mistakes/
7. Taylor, B. (2021, September 17). How Coca-Cola, Netflix, and Amazon learn from failure. *Harvard Business Review*. https://hbr.org/2017/11/how-coca-cola-netflix-and-amazon-learn-from-failure
8. Massicotte, E. (2017, November 14). Your kids are going to do things they shouldn't. It helps if you married someone with a sense of humour. Pic.Twitter.Com/Vvtstejbjo. Twitter, *November 14, 2017*. https://twitter.com/DrMassicotte/status/930225763638317058

Chapter 4

1. Rozin, P., & Royzman, E.B. (2001). Negativity bias, negativity dominance, and contagion. *Personality and Social Psychology Review*, *5*(4), 296–320.

2. American Physiological Society. (2008, April 10). Anticipating a laugh reduces our stress hormones, study shows. ScienceDaily. https://www.sciencedaily.com/releases/2008/04/080407114617.htm
3. Cheng, D., & Wang, L. (2015). Examining the energizing effects of humor: The influence of humor on persistence behavior. *Journal of Business and Psychology*, *30*(4), 759–772.
4. Zander-Schellenberg, T., Collins, I.M., Miché, M., Guttmann, C., Lieb, R., & Wahl, K. (2020). Does laughing have a stress-buffering effect in daily life? An intensive longitudinal study. *PLOS One*, *15*(7): e0235851. https://doi.org/10.1371/journal.pone.0235851
5. Baumeister, R.F., Vohs, K.D., & Tice, D.M. (2007). The strength model of self-control. *Current Directions in Psychological Science*, *16*(6), 351–355.
6. Marmolejo-Ramos, F., Murata, A., Sasaki, K., Yamada, Y., Ikeda, A., Hinojosa, J.A., Watanabe, K., Parzuchowski, M., Tirado, C., & Ospina, R. (2020). Your face and moves seem happier when I smile. *Experimental Psychology*, *67*, (1), 14–22. https://doi.org/10.1027/1618-3169/a000470
7. Gonot-Schoupinsky, F.N., & Garip, G. (2019). Prescribing laughter to increase well-being in healthy adults: An exploratory mixed methods feasibility study of the Laughie. *European Journal of Integrative Medicine*, *26*, 56–64. https://doi.org/10.1016/j.eujim.2019.01.005

Chapter 5

1. Cherry, K. (n.d.). How priming affects the psychology of memory. Verywell Mind. Retrieved June 7, 2022, from https://www.verywellmind.com/priming-and-the-psychology-of-memory-4173092
2. Wellenzohn, S., Proyer, R.T., & Ruch, W. (2018). Who benefits from humor-based positive psychology interventions? *Frontiers in Psychology*, *9*, 821.
3. Brennan, D. (2021, October 25). How journaling can help ease anxiety and encourage healing. WebMD. Retrieved June 21, 2022, from https://www.webmd.com/mental-health/mental-health-benefits-of-journaling
4. Bryant, F.B., & Veroff, J. (2007). *Savoring: A new model of positive experience.* Lawrence Erlbaum Associates, Publishers.

5. Speer, M.E., & Delgado, M.R. (2017). Reminiscing about positive memories buffers acute stress responses. *Nature Human Behaviour*, *1*(5), 0093. https://doi.org/10.1038/s41562-017-0093
6. Raypole, C. (2020, August 18). Mantra meditation: Benefits, how to try it, and more. Healthline. Retrieved November 28, 2022, from https://www.healthline.com/health/mantra-meditation
7. Amir, O., & Biederman, I. (2016). The neural correlates of humor creativity. *Frontiers in Human Neuroscience*, *10*, 597.
8. Samson, A.C., & Gross, J.J. (2012) Humour as emotion regulation: The differential consequences of negative versus positive humour. *Cognition and Emotion*, *26*(2), 375–384, doi:10.1080/02699931.2011.585069
9. Cann, A., & Collette, C. (2014). Sense of humor, stable affect, and psychological well-being. *Europe's Journal of Psychology*, *10*(3), 464–479. https://doi.org/10.5964/ejop.v10i3.746
10. Hebb, D.O. (2005). *The organization of behavior: A neuropsychological theory*. New York: Psychology Press.

Part 1

1. Curtis, G. (2023, March 31). Our life in numbers: How long we sleep, work & more: Dreams. The Sleep Matters Club. https://www.dreams.co.uk/sleep-matters-club/your-life-in-numbers-infographic
2. Smith, J. (2022, October 12). 10 reasons why humor is a key to success at work. *Forbes*. https://www.forbes.com/sites/jacquelynsmith/2013/05/03/10-reasons-why-humor-is-a-key-to-success-at-work/?sh=16900be35c90
3. Oswald, A.J., Proto, E., & Sgroi, D. (2015). Happiness and productivity. *Journal of Labor Economics*, 33(4), 789–822. https://doi.org/10.1086/681096

Chapter 6

1. Smithsonian Center for Learning and Digital Access. (n.d.). Smithsonian in your classroom: Abraham Lincoln: The face of a war. Smithsonian Education—Welcome. https://smithsonianeducation.org/educators/lesson_plans/lincoln/

2. Thomas, B.P. (1981, January 1). Lincoln's humor: An analysis. Papers of the Abraham Lincoln Association. https://quod.lib.umich.edu/j/jala/2629860.0003.105/--lincoln-s-humor-an-analysis?rgn=main%3Bview
3. *Harvard Business Review*. (2018, February 12). The tough work of turning around a team. *Harvard Business Review*. https://hbr.org/2000/11/the-tough-work-of-turning-around-a-team
4. Hoption, C., Barling, J., & Turner, N. (2013). "It's not you, it's me": Transformational leadership and self-deprecating humor. *Leadership & Organization Development Journal*, 34(1), 4–19. https://doi.org/10.1108/01437731311289947
5. Martin, R.A., Puhlik-Doris, P., Larsen, G., Gray, J., & Weir, K. (2003). Individual differences in uses of humor and their relation to psychological well-being: Development of the humor styles questionnaire. *Journal of Research in Personality*, 37(1), 48–75. https://doi.org/10.1016/s0092-6566(02)00534-2
6. Swann, E. (2022, September 4). Amazon head honcho Jeff Bezos recalls giving notes on LOTR: The rings of power series and has a funny, self-deprecating take. CINEMABLEND. https://www.cinemablend.com/streaming-news/amazon-head-honcho-jeff-bezos-recalls-giving-notes-on-lotr-the-rings-of-power-series-and-has-a-funny-self-deprecating-take
7. Kapur, S. (2023, July 27). How self-deprecating jokes can backfire. *Business Insider*. https://www.businessinsider.com/how-self-deprecation-can-backfire-2013-11

Chapter 7

1. OpenAI. (2023). ChatGPT (Aug 9 version) [Large language model]. https://chat.openai.com/

Chapter 8

1. Amire, R. (n.d.). Fun drives high levels of well-being at the best workplaces for millennials. Great Place To Work®. Accessed August 10, 2023, from https://www.greatplacetowork.com/resources/blog/fun-drives-high-levels-of-well-being-at-the-best-workplaces-for-millennials

2. Nelson, B. (2022, May 2). Why work should be fun. *Harvard Business Review*. https://hbr.org/2022/05/why-work-should-be-fun
3. *Smithsonian Magazine*. (2010, June 1). Madeleine Albright on her life in pins. Smithsonian.com. https://www.smithsonianmag.com/arts-culture/madeleine-albright-on-her-life-in-pins-149191/
4. Trougakos, J.P., Hideg, I., Hayden Cheng, B., & Beal, D.J. (2014). Lunch breaks unpacked: The role of autonomy as a moderator of recovery during lunch. *Academy of Management Journal*, *57*(2), 405–421. https://doi.org/10.5465/amj.2011.1072
5. Gianoulis, N. (2022, April 15). The laws of fun. The Fun Dept. https://thefundept.com/the-laws-of-fun/
6. Plester, B., & Hutchison, A. (2016). Fun times: The relationship between fun and workplace engagement. *Employee Relations*, *38*(3), 332–350. https://doi.org/10.1108/er-03-2014-0027
7. Berns, G.S., McClure, S.M., Pagnoni, G., & Montague, P. (2001). Predictability modulates human brain response to reward. *The Journal of Neuroscience*, *21*(8), 2793–2798. https://doi.org/10.1523/jneurosci.21-08-02793.2001
8. Amabile, T.M. (2020, May 6). The power of small wins. https://hbr.org/2011/05/the-power-of-small-wins
9. Bullock, M. (2023, April 28). Top 10 ways to gamify your company. Spinify. https://spinify.com/blog/gamification-in-training/
10. Hinds, R. (n.d.). The surprising science of having "fun" at Work|Inc. Com. Accessed August 13, 2023, from https://www.inc.com/rebecca-hinds/the-surprising-science-of-having-fun-at-work.html
11. Fessler, L. (2017, June 26). One tiny detail at companies like SpaceX, Google, and Airbnb speaks volumes about their culture. Quartz. https://qz.com/1008140/one-tiny-detail-at-companies-like-spacex-google-and-airbnb-speaks-volumes-about-their-culture
12. Frisch, B., and Greene, C. (2017, September 27). The right way to cut people off in meetings. *Harvard Business Review*. https://hbr.org/2016/04/the-right-way-to-cut-people-off-in-meetings
13. Team building activities on Zoom, teams & Webex. Funtivity. Accessed August 14, 2023, from https://www.funtivity.co/
14. Parra, M. (2015, November 1). Having fun at work? Thank your CEO. https://www.miamiherald.com/news/business/biz-monday/article42037956.html

15. Team, Glassdoor. (2021, May 12). Fun & engaging new hire onboarding ideas. Glassdoor. https://www.glassdoor.com/employers/blog/employees-really-want-onboarding/
16. How Warby Parker makes every point in its employee lifecycle extraordinary. First Round Review. Accessed August 15, 2023, from https://review.firstround.com/how-warby-parker-makes-every-point-in-its-employee-lifecycle-extraordinary

Chapter 9

1. Dcunha, S.D. (2022, June 28). About The, and More. The business case for humor at the workplace. Is the Middle East open to laughs? Fast Company Middle East | The future of tech, business and innovation. https://fastcompanyme.com/work-life/the-business-case-for-humor-at-the-workplace-is-the-middle-east-open-to-laughs/
2. Sinek, S. (2017). *Leaders eat last*. London: Portfolio Penguin.
3. Hansen, B. (2019, November 20). Funny, weird and just plain awesome job descriptions. Work + Money. https://www.workandmoney.com/s/funny-awesome-job-descriptions-12efb939db4641bf
4. Job search | indeed. Accessed August 25, 2023, from https://www.indeed.com/
5. Job search | indeed. Accessed August 25, 2023, from https://www.indeed.com/
6. Hansen, B. (2019, November 20). Funny, weird and just plain awesome job descriptions. Work + Money. https://www.workandmoney.com/s/funny-awesome-job-descriptions-12efb939db4641bf
7. Hansen, B. (2019, November 20). Funny, weird and just plain awesome job descriptions. Work + Money. https://www.workandmoney.com/s/funny-awesome-job-descriptions-12efb939db4641bf
8. Job search | indeed. Accessed August 25, 2023, from https://www.indeed.com/
9. Turner, M. (2023, March 6). National Park Service on Instagram. Instagram. https://www.instagram.com/p/CpeI8NcDKnd/
10. Mandese, J. (2020, February 4). Hyundai's "Smaht Pahk" wins Purchase Intent Bowl, see the other top 10 here. https://www.mediapost.com/

publications/article/346638/hyundais-smaht-pahk-wins-purchase-intent-bowl.html?edition=

11. Rubin, G. (2022). Humor and Happiness Global Research Study. Oracle. https://www.oracle.com/cx/happiness/?source=%3Aow%3Ao%3Abl%3Amt%3A%3A%3APressReleaseProductPage
12. President Barack Obama: Between two ferns with Zach Galifianakis. (2014, March 13). YouTube. https://www.youtube.com/watch?v=UnW3xkHxIEQ
13. Elizabeth Banks in "Just a Little Heart Attack." (2012, March 20). YouTube. https://www.youtube.com/watch?v=_JI487DlgTA
14. Hesterberg, K. (2021, June 11). 7 brands already using chatbots in their marketing. HubSpot Blog. https://blog.hubspot.com/marketing/brands-already-using-chatbots-in-their-marketing
15. Lally, M. (n.d.). 9 of the greatest unsubscribe page examples you can steal. Accessed September 1, 2023, from https://www.bluleadz.com/blog/unsubscribe-page-examples
16. Traveler. Dollar Shave Club. Accessed September 1, 2023, from https://us.dollarshaveclub.com/products/traveler

Chapter 10

1. Sus, V. (2016, January 16). "All I know is that I know nothing": What did Socrates mean? TheCollector. https://www.thecollector.com/all-i-know-is-that-i-know-nothing-socrates/
2. Gibbs, A. (2022, April 4). Boss pretending to fire employee as April Fools sparks backlash online. *Newsweek*. https://www.newsweek.com/boss-pretending-fire-employee-april-fools-backlash-online-1694619
3. Hagen, A. (2012, March 20). Bell Leadership Study finds humor gives leaders the edge. Business Wire. https://www.businesswire.com/news/home/20120320005971/en/Bell-Leadership-Study-Finds-Humor-Gives-Leaders-the-Edge
4. Associated Press. (2023, May 9). ESPN anchor apologizes to Zach Whitecloud for mocking name. ESPN. https://www.espn.com/nhl/story/_/id/37591759/espn-anchor-apologizes-zach-whitecloud-mocking-name

Chapter 11

1. Senz, K. (2022, March 24). Rituals at work: Teams that play together stay together. HBS Working Knowledge. https://hbswk.hbs.edu/item/rituals-at-work-teams-that-play-together-stay-together
2. Senz, K. (2022, March 24). Rituals at work: Teams that play together stay together. HBS Working Knowledge. https://hbswk.hbs.edu/item/rituals-at-work-teams-that-play-together-stay-togethe
3. Allan, B.A., Batz-Barbarich, C., Sterling, H.M., & Tay, L. (2018). Outcomes of meaningful work: A meta-analysis. *Journal of Management Studies, 56*(3), 500–528. https://doi.org/10.1111/joms.12406
4. Kim, T., Sezer, O., Schroeder, J., Risen, J., Gino, F., & Norton, M.I. (2021). Work group rituals enhance the meaning of work. *Organizational Behavior and Human Decision Processes, 165*. 197–212. https://doi.org/10.1016/j.obhdp.2021.05.005
5. Achor, S. (2011). *The happiness advantage*. Random House.
6. Washut, K. (n.d.). Core value #10: Have fun: Far reach blog. Far Reach. Accessed September 12, 2023, from https://www.farreachinc.com/blog/core-value-10-have-fun
7. Jackson, A. (2020, April 12). Here's how hospitals are celebrating when a Covid-19 patient is released. CNN. https://www.cnn.com/2020/04/12/health/covid-19-patient-released-celebration-trnd-wellness/index.html

Chapter 12

1. Ostrower, C. (2015). Humor as a defense mechanism during the Holocaust. *Interpretation: A Journal of Bible and Theology, 69*(2), 183–195. https://doi.org/10.1177/0020964314564830
2. Sultanoff, S.M. (2008, March). Humor therapy. Humor Therapy in Today's Woman of Orange County. https://www.humormatters.com/articles/HumorTherapy2008.htm
3. Barry, D. (2002, August 18). Wash anxiety. *Washington Post*. https://www.washingtonpost.com/archive/lifestyle/magazine/2002/08/18/wash-anxiety/9c08021d-d973-433b-b535-e9da64392545/

Acknowledgments

Kelly, thank you for your unconditional support of my lunacy and for laughing even when you've heard it a million times. You are what inspires me to do anything great. Bridger, thank you for being the best writing partner and best friend. Edwin, thank you for making me laugh every day. Hipple, get off the keyboard—I'm writingggggg

Mom, thank you for showing me how to be smart before being a smart ass. Ali and Laurie, thank you for not letting me take myself too seriously, and for a lifetime of absolute goofiness. Dad, thank you for believing in me, the ability to make funny faces, and never having to worry about doing my hair. Dave L., thank you for always laughing, oh, and . . . you're a good cook! Dave F., thank you for always making me laugh, but quit being funnier than me. Brian, thank you for your under-the-breath, well-timed dry wit. Haile, Hannah, Scott, and Alison—thank you for being the best kids I never had and more importantly . . . funny. Jar, thank you for keeping me grounded and always having my back—oh, and good call. I love you all.

Thank you to my agent, Leah Spiro, for believing in me and this book. Thank you, Ruth Mills. Thank you to the entire Wiley team, including Brian Neill, Gabriela Manusco, Deborah Schindlar, and Julie Kerr, for helping me get this book out to the world.

Chris, thank you for teaching me to fish and being my humor sounding board. Dale and Megan, thank you for putting up with me through college and supporting my early comedy career and delusions of grandeur.

Last Best Comedy, thank you for being the (last) best humor playground and a needed outlet for me and an entire community.

Thank you to my friends at the Association for Applied and Therapeutic Humor (AATH): Jennifer Keith, Mallori DeSalle, Heidi Hanna, and Michele St. Clair. Thank you, Karyn Buxman, for your wisdom, leadership, and inspiration in the field of applied humor.

Marilyn and Mark Oestreicher, thank you for letting me highlight Amy's beautiful spirit. Casey S., thank you for always laughing at my jokes and for your story in this book. Jake H., thank you for your service—primarily to the country, but also to this book.

Jenn Lim and the entire Delivering Happiness crew, thank you for your trust in me and making the world happier. Thank you to all the staff and students I've worked with at the University of Northern Colorado, Front Range Community College, The University of California, Riverside, Colorado State University, The Culinary Institute of America, and Community Matters.

About the Author

Paul Osincup is a Keynote Speaker, Corporate Trainer, and Comedian who uses the science of happiness and applied humor to help people and organizations thrive.

Paul's global mission for workplace happiness has provided him the opportunity to speak to hundreds of organizations, including the U.S. Army, the Harvard Kennedy School of Leadership, Google, and Discover. Paul is a TEDx speaker, a trainer with international work culture experts Delivering Happiness, and a content creator for the mental health and well-being app Happify.

Paul is past president of the Association for Applied and Therapeutic Humor, a nonprofit organization dedicated to the study and application of humor to enhance health, well-being, and performance. He's also past president of his elementary school student council.

Paul's work has been highlighted in the *New York Times*, *Forbes*, and on his mom's refrigerator.

Connect with Paul:

Website: paulosincup.com

Social media: @paulosincup (, , , , , and)

Index